FEMINIST *AF*

FEMINIST AF

A GUIDE TO CRUSHING GIRLHOOD

BRITTNEY COOPER

CHANEL CRAFT TANNER

SUSANA MORRIS

NORTON YOUNG READERS

An Imprint of W. W. Norton & Company · Independent Publishers Since 1923

Lucille Clifton, excerpt from "*won't you celebrate with me*" from *The Book of Light.*
Copyright © 1993 by Lucille Clifton. Reprinted with the permission of
The Permissions Company, LLC, on behalf of Copper Canyon Press,
coppercanyonpress.org.

For information about permission to reproduce selections from this book, write to
Permissions, W. W. Norton & Company, Inc., 500 Fifth Avenue, New York, NY 10110

For information about special discounts for bulk purchases, please contact
W. W. Norton Special Sales at specialsales@wwnorton.com or 800-233-4830

Manufacturing by Versa Press
Book design by Monique Sterling
Production manager: Anna Oler

ISBN 978-1-324-00505-6 (pbk.)

W. W. Norton & Company, Inc.
500 Fifth Avenue, New York, N.Y. 10110
wwnorton.com

W. W. Norton & Company Ltd.
15 Carlisle Street, London W1D 3BS

2 4 6 8 9 0 7 5 3 1

For Tiana, Joseph, Na'im, Cori, Cairo, and Asali,
and all our little sisters and sibs everywhere

CONTENTS _____

FEMINIST *AF*

LET'S GET IT STARTED

WHO IS THIS BOOK FOR? _____

We wrote this book for all the girls who proudly rep the feminist flag but want to know how to live their feminism out loud. We packed it full of things you should know on your journey to feminism. It will help you grapple with friendships, bodies, family dynamics, emotional health, music, misogyny, racism, pop culture, and more. This book is for loud and rowdy girls (*turn down for what?!*), quiet and nerdy girls, girls who rock naturals, girls who wear weaves, outspoken girls, opinionated girls, girls still finding their voice, girls who are already feminists and girls who don't know what feminism is, queer girls, trans girls, and gender nonbinary young folks who want to make the world better and who need the insights feminism has to make it happen.

Everyone has something to say about girls. They're too thick, too sexual, too bossy, too quiet, too loud, too fast, too everything. It's all too much. How can you love yourself, be yourself, and advocate for yourself and others when everyone tries to make you feel like you're a problem? Well, we're here to tell you that feminism can help you address almost any question that will shape your life. We wrote this book to give you tips, strategies, and resources, to show you what feminism looks like in real life, and to help answer many of the questions you may have on your road to crushing girlhood.

Questions like: How do you give yourself compassion and grace in a world that tells you you're not enough? How can you use feminism to build your confidence and leadership abilities? How do you stand up for yourself and own your power and your voice? And how do you deal with the burden of the expectation of Black girl resiliency while also celebrating #BlackGirlMagic? In the first section of this book, "Me, Myself, and I," we show you how feminism can help you with self-love, self-confidence, and self-assurance, and offer you a notion of collective well-being.

Maybe your questions are about crushing beauty goals while feminist. You may be asking: What do you do when you don't like your natural hair, or when people won't stop talking about it? What is body positivity, and is it available to you as a trans girl when it seems the world demands you can't be who you are? How do you address colorism and beauty privilege in a family and culture that may prize fair-skinned women over those with darker skin tones? How do you dress and present yourself in ways that feel good to you? Our "Beauty" section has many of the answers you're looking for.

We know that family issues and expectations, friendships, and dating are also big deals for young women, so the "What About Your Friends (and Family and 'Em)?" section covers those issues. You're getting older and as the relationship with your family changes, you may be wondering if feminism can help you navigate these new dynamics. How do you figure out which version of you is the real one, the one with your parents or the one with your friends? How do you actually date while feminist? And what about sex? Is feminist sex a thing? And how can feminism help you navigate some of the issues you're having with your homegirls and help you build meaningful friendships? We got you.

You may have heard of intersectionality but are wondering what it looks like to practice a feminist politics that includes all kinds of women. How does wealth inequality intersect with feminism? What if you're an immigrant or the child of immigrants, and you have all this cultural pressure to meet your parents' expectations while feeling like you just don't fit in anywhere you go? How do you crush girlhood in the face of racism? How do you figure out the kind of physical and emotional intimacy you want to have with others while exploring your sexuality? No worries, we keep it real about classism, code-switching, white supremacy, and homophobia in "Fight the Power," and then wrap it up with some final thoughts about how you can use your feminism to make a difference in the world.

We got you, little sis. Given all the noise it can be hard to figure out who you even are and what things you care about. Feminism can help you to clear out some of the clutter and figure out what things matter to you. We've been there and we have some tips to help you crush girlhood, feminist-style. We love feminism, and we believe it offers you a world of possibilities when it comes to what's important to you and what's good for you.

A FEW KEY CONCEPTS

Before we go any further, there are a few concepts we need to go over, because they will come up quite frequently throughout the book.

Oppression

Oppression is a strong word, and we know it. But when folks with power and privilege—usually straight people, white folks, men, cisgender people, the rich, the First World, and the able-bodied—use their power to keep anybody who is not like them from winning, that is a system of oppression. By "winning," we mean that they hoard access to good jobs, great schools, and safe neighborhoods, and create a world where those things are difficult to obtain if you aren't white or rich. It is important to remember that we aren't talking about anyone being an individual oppressor. We are talking about how the world is set up to work for people who fit into certain categories and to disadvantage those who don't.

Socialization

Gender is a social construct. It's not something that just happens naturally. From the time your parents throw a "gender reveal" party (I mean, it's really a genital reveal, because you haven't even gotten here yet, and you haven't even chosen your gender yet!) or the moment they start painting the nursery in pink for girls and blue for boys, a gender story is being created that you are supposed to map onto your body. For a lot of people, the gender story mostly works. But for some people, the gender story doesn't work at all. They know it because something feels wrong—not with them, but with what other people are telling them about who they are.

For instance, we are told that girls are naturally more emotional than boys. If you have ever hung out with babies, you know that boy babies (or rather, babies that we think will grow up to be boys) have plenty of emotions. Emotions and feelings are not determined by genitals. In fact, not much is determined by genitals. Mostly, your genitalia tell us something about how your body might reproduce and how it might experience sexual pleasure. But those things don't tell us very much at all about what your gender should be or who you might someday like or fall in love with or have sex with.

When you fall in line with what is prescribed for your gender, you get rewarded. But what if you just can't make yourself do the things the script tells you to? What if you're a boy who plays dress-up, or you're a girl who prefers to play football? What if you can tell that your parents or grandparents or aunts and uncles and cousins are embarrassed by the things you feel comfortable doing? What if the kids in your class call you weird and avoid you, and the adults in your life start apologizing for your behavior? This is how the gender-socialization train starts. You are given models to follow, and when you don't, other kids and adults communicate that you're doing it wrong.

What's natural is you picking the toy you want to play with. What's social is everything everyone has to say about it, and what's completely messed up is the way you get treated when you do something outside the norm. You experience the world like this enough before age five, and before long, you'll be following gender scripts and thinking that this is just how things are supposed to be.

But feminism says, "Eff that!" Genitals are not destiny, and gender is what you make it. But it also says that we will not stand for a world in which little girls, and later women, are bossed around by men simply because they are girls. That's not how this works. That's not how any of this works! Feminism also says that however you come to your girlhood or your womanhood is just fine with us—whether you are a trans girl, a cis girl, a gender nonbinary femme, whatever pronouns you rock—it's all good! There's room for you here.

Feminism

Feminism is about freedom. It is a movement that says your gender and your biological sex should not determine your destiny. It is a movement to end oppression on the basis of gender toward women and girls, trans people, and gender nonbinary people.

When we say "Smash the patriarchy!" this is what we mean: destroy the system that imposes gender on people, hates girls and women, and tells men to be leaders even when they are mediocre AF. That system makes it hard for everybody who is not a cisgender white male to live and thrive.

Oh yeah . . . we probably need to define "the patriarchy," because that's what this book is really about. Getting rid of his bum ass. Feminist movements are a response to a system of power that we call patriarchy. Patriarchy is a system that assumes that men, particularly cisgender, white, heterosexual, able-bodied men, should be leaders simply because they are men. Many of our oldest social institutions, from the Church to our government, have presumed that the world is set up for men to lead. Some scientists like to argue that this is simply a function of evolution. They claim that since men were the hunters many thousands of years ago in prehistoric communities, that they are "naturally" supposed to lead. We already told you about how we feel about "natural." Feminism says, "Get that ish TF outta here. We can build a world where gender is a resource, not a barrier."

Black/Women of Color Feminism

Feminism is great and all, but it's only truly great when it figures out how to hold the truth of *all* women. Our feminism unapologetically begins with the story of how women of color, Black, Brown, and Indigenous, came to fight the patriarchy.

In 1831, a Black female abolitionist named Maria Stewart started giving lectures to audiences of Black and white men and women, about the need to end slavery. In every lecture, she advocated for the rights specifically of Black women and girls, both those who were enslaved and those who were technically free but still struggling. She was the first woman on record of any race to do this. So when we claim feminism for ourselves, we do it in the name of women like Maria Stewart, sisters who understood that in order for Black women to be free, you had to combat poverty, sexism, and white supremacy. We do it in the name of Gloria Anzaldúa, a pioneering Chicana feminist, who taught us about how the borderlands that cause so much trouble for our Chicanx folks in the United States can teach us new ways to do our feminism.

When white feminists tell the story of feminism, they rarely begin with women of color. They say U.S. feminism really began at Seneca Falls, New York, in 1848, when a group of white women, including Susan B. Anthony and Elizabeth Cady Stanton, got together and declared that women have rights. The problem is that Indigenous and Black women had been fighting for their rights since white male colonizers showed up on the shores of the Americas to steal Indigenous lands and showed up on the shores of Africa to steal Africans to work those stolen lands. Indigenous women customarily had tribal rights. They could vote in tribal councils, serve in leadership roles, and divorce their husbands.

White women like Sarah and Angelina Grimké and working-class white women mill workers in 1830s Massachusetts played an important role in advancing the cause of feminism, but they didn't invent it. And they don't own it.

We're keeping it real about this not because we want to alienate our white women allies. We don't. There's all kinds of cool feminist, antiracist white women and girl allies, past and present—folks like Lucy Stone, Ashley Judd, Megan Rapinoe, Greta Thunberg, and Emma Watson—who are about this life. We need them in a world

FEMINIST *AF*

filled with unhelpful Karen- and Becky-type energy. We depend on their integrity in a world where white-girl tears—that annoying thing where white women cry when they get called out on their racism—are running rampant.

But Black and Brown girls have often been resistant to claiming feminism, a political stance our Black women ancestors helped to invent, because white girls act like they own it. When we say "girl power!" people are rarely thinking about girls of color.

Our position is that there is room at the table for everybody. Congresswoman Shirley Chisholm famously said that if there were no seats at the table, she would "bring a folding chair." But we can do better than that, can't we? This isn't the 1970s anymore! We can construct new tables.

When Black and Brown girls are at the table, and when they are blowing the bullhorn, and when they are making the room accessible, everybody wins. So if you're down with trying to smash the patriarchy, pull up a chair, roll up your wheelchair, or see the sign interpreter making it clear: There is room for you.

Intersectionality

Just like those Black women abolitionists in the nineteenth century, Black feminists make clear that fighting against gender oppression is not enough. You have to fight against racism and poverty, and every other form of oppression, in order to truly be free.

That's what we mean when we say that feminism must be intersectional. Listen up, we got a story to tell (*cue Biggie*).

Once upon a time, way back in the 1970s, the baddest collective of feminists to ever exist, the Combahee River Collective, said that Black women experienced a "simultaneity of oppressions." They meant that we got hit with the double whammy of white supremacy and sexism at the same damn time. Just because the civil rights and Black Power movements of the 1960s and 1970s had fought to end racial oppression, it didn't mean that Black women would automatically be free. Black women had to fight really hard to be allowed to speak at the March on Washington for Jobs and Freedom, that same march where Dr. Martin Luther King gave his "I Have a Dream" speech. And the number of Black women who got to say something was still paltry in comparison to the scores of men.

Meanwhile, the feminist movements that were budding at the time were often focused primarily on white women and their desires to build careers outside the home and to not only have to focus on mothering their children. Black households were different: They were always two-income households because that's the only way Black families could be economically self-sufficient. Moreover, many Black women did domestic labor in white homes, even as white women complained about being bored housewives. We all needed feminist struggle, but we needed it for different reasons.

A dope Black feminist, attorney, and professor named Kimberlé Crenshaw invented the term "intersectionality" as a way to name Black women's experience of being oppressed both because we are Black and female, and often because we are poor. Crenshaw said that you could only understand our experience by looking at the *intersection* of these structural conditions: racism and sexism.

Have y'all seen those stories about how braids are prohibited in a school's dress code? This is an example of why intersectionality is important. Braids are an ethnic hairstyle worn frequently by Black girls, because they are low-maintenance and versatile. When a school dress code targets that style, it is discriminating against Black girls—not all girls, and not all Black people. Intersectionality helps us to name those forms of discrimination and power that happen at the intersection of two systems. In the case of the braids, to simply call the policy sexist would be to miss the ways it doesn't target all girls. To simply call the policy racist would miss the ways it doesn't target all people of color. If we use what we call an *intersectional lens*, it becomes clear that even when school rules don't say anything explicit about racism or sexism, they can still negatively affect Black girls.

What about your undocumented homegirl who wants you to go with her to Planned Parenthood for a conversation on birth-control options? What happens when you discover, as happened in Tennessee, that there is a branch of Immigration and Customs Enforcement (ICE) in the same building as Planned Parenthood? Suddenly, going to get routine medical care becomes scary if you're a young, undocumented woman of color, because you might get apprehended and deported.

Since oppression is intersectional, feminism has to be too. The great thing is that anybody can be an intersectional feminist. You don't have to be Black or Brown to understand that Black and Latinx and Asian American Pacific Islander (AAPI) and Indigenous women and girls experience sexism, racism, and poverty differently depending on how their experiences and identities intersect. You simply have to be committed to fighting for freedom for everybody, while respecting what each of these groups says freedom means for them.

Feminism and Decolonization

Maybe you've heard people say that those of us socialized under white supremacy and patriarchy need to decolonize our minds. That means that we need to mentally undo all the terrible things we believe about race, gender, our bodies, and our relationships, bequeathed to us courtesy of systems that don't love us.

But we use the term "decolonize" as a way to recognize that the modern world was created when European men from places like Portugal, Spain, the Netherlands, France, and Britain began to travel around the world "discovering"—ahem, stealing—Indigenous lands for themselves and turning them into colonies. These men also traveled to West Africa and stole African laborers to cultivate these lands.

Decolonization isn't just about learning to love yourself. That matters. But colonization happened to real people who lived in actual places. Decolonization will have to happen there too. Part of what it means to undo the terrible and unhelpful ways we think about gender is always to remember how we got here in the first place. What Native peoples used to live on the land you now live on? How did they think about gender? What kind of tribal rights did the women who lived there have? How are local Indigenous communities around your way faring today? They teach us that there are other ways of being and existing in relation to the land. Patriarchy isn't the only way. So as we decolonize, we remember that there are always other ways to live in this world, and some of those ways are more equitable and hospitable to people of color, queer people, and trans and gender nonbinary people.

WHO IS WRITING THIS BOOK?

We want you to imagine us as your big sisters or aunties, here to give you a little bit of guidance about how we actually apply feminism. We are three Black women who used to be Black girls. We have been where you are, faced the same challenges with dating, friendships, and our bodies. We want you to believe us when we say we got you, so we're going to tell you a bit about ourselves and our own journeys into feminism.

Brittney's Story

I didn't start calling myself a feminist until I was twenty-three years old and taking a graduate school course on race and feminism. Up until then, I had never paid attention to the operations of patriarchy, because I thought women ran everything. My grandmother, my mother, and her sisters, my aunts, kept our family together. I mostly thought of the men—my uncles, my cousins, and my own father, who struggled with addiction—as knuckleheads who couldn't get their lives together. In fact, I told my Girl Scout troop leader exactly this one day, when I was about eight years old: "Boys are nothing but trouble."

I also loved and pursued friendships with other girls. I had a clear but distinct sense, really from those earliest days in Girl Scouts, that having rich, abiding friendships with girls was a lifeline I needed. Perhaps my love of the Baby-Sitters Club book series shaped my thinking about friendship. Or maybe it was that my mother always had homegirls, Black and white, rolling through our house, keeping things lit with laughter and tall tales. What I knew for sure was that I needed homegirls of my own, because boys were not to be trusted with your deep, secret things.

So, the idea that the women in my life were oppressed by some system of male dominance seemed not to fit. But later, I came to realize how the knuckleheadedness and dysfunction of all these men took up all the space in the room. How we spent inordinate amounts of time as a family cleaning up messes these men made, due in no small part to their own investments in ideas of masculinity that didn't serve them well. I came to recognize the way that my father's violent acts against my mother had indelibly shaped both her life and mine, the way his violent explosions had harmed my sense of safety, the ways his chaos had tried to make our world small. But I also saw and deeply admired the way my mother pushed back, refusing his artificial limits in her choice to keep dreaming and working toward something better.

Black women have always been my lifeline and my safe haven. But when I was nine years old, I didn't know to call that feminism. I didn't learn the language about how patriarchy acts through violence to control and limit women's life possibilities until I was much older. And I didn't realize until I was twenty-three that although I loved learning about Black history, most of the figures I had learned about, save the inimitable Rosa Parks, whom I played in the fourth-grade class play, were men. That, too, was patriarchy: this idea that every great thing ever done in history was done by a man first. And then I came to realize how much I needed feminism to understand my own life, filled as it was with women who made magic with very few resources every single day while getting little to no credit for doing any of it. If we are not careful, we will continue to build the world that way, on the backs of strong women who show up even when it's inconvenient to do the labor, even when they are asked to do more than their fair share, all the while paying them less, protecting them less, and recognizing them insufficiently.

I am a feminist because I want a different life for myself and other women and girls, one where my choices and options are not limited by the screw-ups of men, one where women and girls are celebrated fully, in their humanity and complexity and messiness, and one where we are truly able to see, appreciate, and rock out for one another.

Chanel's Story

I didn't hear the word "feminism" until taking my first women's studies course in college, but once I heard it I quickly gravitated to the idea. Even though I wasn't a feminist until I was eighteen, there were little feminist seeds being planted all along.

First, I grew up in a predominantly woman-run family. My mother was one of three daughters born to a mother who was one of four daughters. Because there were no boys around, my mother and my grandmother were expected to do things that were seen as traditional boy roles. My mother took out the trash and cooked dinner. My grandmother learned to sew and fix things around the house. All this made me incredibly receptive to the notion of women's equality and made me reject the idea that there were "natural" roles for women and men.

When I was about ten years old, I fell in love with hip-hop. Knowing the words to all the hit songs would solidify your spot in the popular circle. I spent evenings with my cassette player, pen, and paper, pressing Stop, Pause, and Rewind to get down the lyrics to the brand-new Biggie song or memorize the bars to Method Man and Mary J's rendition of "You're All I Need." I was often the lone girl on the stoop debating the flows of Biggie, Jay Z, and Nas. This made it easy for me to understand misogyny and the objectification of women when I learned these concepts in college. I was silenced when the conversation would center on sex (and since I was in middle school, that's pretty much where the conversations always went). Hip-hop had a very clear place for women: as objects who exist for the purposes of pleasing men in one way or another.

Then Lil' Kim burst onto the scene—legs wide open, staring directly at the camera, ready to take hip-hop by storm. For me and my homegirls, Lil' Kim represented the ability to talk back and declare that her body was hers. She represented agency, bodily autonomy, and sex positivity. She taught me that I could be in control of my own body and that women should expect and demand pleasure in sex.

So, by the time I got to that women's studies class, I had already experienced my fair share of sexism. At that time, I was an engineering major, one of only four girls in my entire section. And while the boys would share answers and strategies across groups, our attempts to get help would be met with disdain. At the same time, I was taking that incredible class where I was learning all the ways that women are oppressed, and I was experiencing sexism firsthand. I always knew I was Black, and the ways in which race and racism would affect my life. However, I did not really realize how being a girl was doing the same thing. That first women's studies class was where I opened my eyes to the gendered division of labor in my father's household, where I washed the dishes and my brother mowed the grass. I saw how it influenced my dating life, where it was expected that the boys would holler and the girls would play hard to get. It even influenced the resources our sports teams received, because as cheerleaders we had to fundraise and/or pay out of pocket for our uniforms and supplies every year, while the boys had everything covered. I was becoming increasingly aware of sexism, and it blew my mind.

The feminism I was learning about was deeply concerned with race. It had a sharp critique of capitalism, helping us to understand why the poor get poorer and the rich get richer. And it expanded my ideas of justice, moving me from just wanting to punish people for doing harmful stuff to wanting restorative justice—a community-based way for those who did the harm to try to repair it. It was a feminism that was first and foremost rooted in a deep love for people and supported the idea that we need to completely restructure our way of being and build a new world that is centered on people of color.

Feminism guides my friendships, structures my marriage, and influences the way I raise my children. I am a proud feminist, and I'm so glad I made the decision to become one all those years ago.

Susana's Story

My earliest introduction to feminism was through my mama—not that she ever used the term. Still, she has always been my feminist role model. Growing up in a strict, religious household during the Great Depression made my mother something of a rebel. She was not allowed to wear pants as a kid because that was a thing that women just did not do. But when she got grown she not only wore pants, she went to a photography studio and did a whole photo shoot wearing them! This may not seem like a big deal today, but back in the day it was a big middle finger to the establishment.

She openly defied the patriarchy every chance she got. She immigrated to the United States from Jamaica by herself, lived alone, married late, and traveled frequently in an era when working-class Black women were expected to get married and have children young. When she did get married, in the 1970s, she wore a white pantsuit and kept her own last name. As a single mother, she always told me and my sisters that women got the short end of the stick in relationships and that marriage was for the birds. She also said women could do anything men can do—drive trucks, pilot planes, be doctors and lawyers. She made it clear that gender was made up and used as an excuse to keep women silent and submissive. She encouraged us to be independent and not rely on a partner to take care of us. She always railed against beauty pageants, even while rooting for Black women to win them (shit is complicated), because she objected to women having to wear a swimsuit to win a scholarship. Sexism worked her last nerve, and she always spoke up about it.

With this sort of model in my house, I was a baby feminist from the jump. I was that girl in school who always had her hand raised and was ready to make her voice heard. Even though I was shy in social situations, I never doubted my intelligence and my right to speak, because my mother instilled that sense of pride in me. In high school, I discovered the nonfiction of Alice Walker. I had already loved *The Color Purple*, but when I read her definition of *womanism* as feminism for Black women and girls, I was all in. It was cool to see what I saw in my mama and her friends defined by an author who spoke to me. I chose to attend a women's college because I wanted to study in an environment that focused on women's education. By the time I got to college and read the works of Patricia Hill Collins and bell hooks, I proudly wore the mantle of Black feminist and have never looked back.

I am a feminist because as a queer Black woman who is the daughter of immigrants, feminism gives me the language to describe and define my own experience. I am a feminist because as a teacher, writer, and community activist I believe the personal is political. Like the writer Toni Cade Bambara taught us, revolution begins within. Feminism is the lens through which I make sense of myself and the world. It helps us understand what's happening but doesn't dictate how we should respond. In the words of hip-hop feminist Joan Morgan, my feminism "fucks with the grays" and is complicated, just as complicated as all the feminists who have shaped me.

WHAT IS CRUNK FEMINISM, AND WHY?————————

We are part of a group of dope-ass women-of-color feminists called the Crunk Feminist Collective, and as our name suggests we see immense value in *collectivity*. A collective is a group of people who come together around a unified goal or purpose. For us, it's to smash the patriarchy! We believe that one of the ways we can do that is by disrupting the idea of individualism. The only way we survive the issues of the world today is by emphasizing community well-being and letting go of an idea of being out for oneself. One person can't take a system down all by herself; you have to have a crew!

So what is "crunk"? You guys are not the first generation to give the side eye to Boomers for many of their ageist antics! Hip-hop, from its very first day, has been a perpetual OK Boomer kinda mood. And we grew up on hip-hop music. It's our soundtrack to love and fun; it's our party music; and with its rampant misogyny and objectification of women and girls, it also politicized us.

We're hip-hop-generation feminists. The soundtrack to our lives isn't the same as the blues, soul, and R&B that our parents and grandparents loved to listen to when we were children. Our music is filled with bass, booties, and plenty of cussing. It is irreverent and just our speed, because trying to be a damn lady has never been the goal of our feminism.

Crunk music is a very particular type of hip-hop music. It's filled with raucous, in-your-face, take-no-prisoners energy, it always gets the party started, and once you've experienced it, you are forever changed. At least, we were. That's also what feminism means to us, a group of Black and Brown women raised on the music that everybody loved to hate for the first two decades of its existence. Hip-hop is ubiquitous now, but it was not always so.

It is music inspired by young men and women who made instruments out of their bodies and busted down doors, demanding to be heard in the face of a government that had decided after the freedom movements of the last century that Black and Brown folks were expendable, and that our lives didn't matter.

Hip-hop, and more specifically crunk music, bounced into the room declaring, "If you don't give a damn, we DGAF!" And when we think of what it means to smash the patriarchy, we are keeping that same energy!

So back in 2010, we formed a group of super-dope women of color called the Crunk Feminist Collective to help us navigate, survive, and wreck shop in our classes, work environments, churches, and even our homes. The three of us are members, and the rest of the crew includes Sheri Davis, a labor organizer and community activist; Rachel Raimist, a media scholar and film director; Eesha Pandit, a political strategist; and Robin Boylorn, a professor of communication studies. We're like the Wu-Tang Clan of feminism—each dope in our own right, but when we link up, we create magic. And we're giving our girls shout-outs, because throughout this book, you'll hear us talk about the importance of having a crew.

We came up on Queen Latifah, MC Lyte, Lauryn Hill, Missy Elliot, Da Brat, Trina, Rasheeda, Mia X, Foxy Brown, and Lil' Kim. If we'd have been so lucky, we would have gone to high school with Beyoncé and Nicki Minaj.

But look, y'all. That's *our* soundtrack. Crunk is our generation's music. It doesn't have to be yours.

I mean, y'all got some sisters out here killing the game right now, and we are here for all of 'em. Cardi B, Megan Thee Stallion (them knees, sis!), Tierra Whack, City Girls, Noname, CHIKA, Lizzo. Y'all's MCs got bars. And your generation has its own sound and its own vibe, its own juice that will power your politics. You and your crew should feel free to remix our shit and create your own feminism relevant to you. It's time.

Feminists have all the tea. We know where all the bodies are buried. We've peeped all the systemic logics that are designed to keep women, girls, and femmes oppressed in the name of shoring up white cisgender male power. If you want to understand why women are paid less and are disproportionately poor around the globe, feminism has the answer. If you wonder why reproductive rights are continually on the chopping block in this country, or why people are being forced to have children that they would otherwise choose not to have, feminism's got the answers. If you wonder why this country struggles to elect a woman to the presidency, whether she is more centrist or more progressive, we feminists have some ideas about why that is. And if you ever asked yourself why we needed a #MeToo movement, we certainly have the cheat code for that one.

It's the patriarchy, dammit. Patriarchy is the system that has led to these terrible conditions for women both in the United States and around the globe. Patriarchy has bequeathed us rape culture, coerced parenthood, slut-shaming, mansplaining, Karens and Beckys in every generation, misogynist music, body hatred, colorism, fat-shaming, you name it.

And it's time for all that shit to come crumbling down. Frederick Douglass, the famous abolitionist who supported women's rights, said "power concedes nothing without a demand. It never has and it never will." Feminism is up for the fight to save our future from the patriarchs and mediocre dudes who think they run this. They don't run shit. We got this, and every smart girl knows: the future is up to us.

Feminism is fun. It makes life better. Don't believe it when people tell you that feminists hate men—shit, we have sons, brothers, fathers, uncles, husbands, and boyfriends too. Don't believe it when they tell you that we ruin all the fun— we watch *Love & Hip Hop* and practice our twerking skills and rap all the lyrics to "Bodak Yellow" too. We can do dance challenges for the 'Gram and TikTokwith the best of 'em. Don't believe it when they say we are only angry—our lives are filled with so much joy and passion and purpose.

And whoever ain't down for the cause can #StayMad about it. We are guided by great feelings of love and hope that we can build a better world for everyone—but we can't do it without our little sisters/siblings!

1

ME, MYSELF, AND I

FLAWLESS

*A*ll day every day, girls get messages about our inferiority. We're too loud, too bossy, too aggressive, too nice, too mean, too fat, too skinny, too opinionated, too shy. Either we're too much, we're told, or not enough. If you're a girl of color, the messages are even more intense. It's exhausting. But here's the thing: It's lies. It's all lies.

You are enough. Full stop. Let's begin there. You are enough even when you don't feel like it. Even when you don't believe it.

We know there are a lot of self-help books you could read about how to love yourself, but the problem with all those books is that they never acknowledge *why* it's so hard for us to love ourselves in the first place. You already know what we're gonna say.

It's the patriarchy, dammit! Yes, it's still the patriarchy. That MF. Patriarchy tells us that our value is based on outward appearance. "Pretty privilege" is a thing. And it works together with racism to promote the most limiting ideas about who is beautiful. The sad reality is that when we feel unattractive, we feel unworthy of being treated with dignity and respect.

But you *are* worthy. Even if you are having a bad hair day. Even if you have acne. Whether you have a big ass or a flat ass. Whether you got big breasts or you're part of the itty-bitty-titty committee. Your worth is not in question.

When we say love yourself, that is what we mean: believing in your own fundamental worthiness and value, in your right to be loved and protected, and treated with kindness and care and compassion.

Self-love is a feminist issue for a couple of reasons. First, as feminists say, the personal is political. By that we mean that our personal experiences and beliefs have political consequences. We live within a series of systems—white supremacy, patriarchy, and capitalism—that work by devaluing people based on race, gender, and capacity to earn money. These systems communicate that only certain people are valuable and lovable. When we are not careful, we can internalize all the lies that the white supremacist capitalist patriarchy (whew, that was a mouthful!) tells us about ourselves. Hating ourselves can become a part of our personal belief system. And you better believe that when we devalue ourselves, that ish has deep political consequences. Part of smashing the patriarchy is recognizing the lie. You are worthy simply because you exist. And in order to effectively fight back against these systems, you've got to believe it.

Second, when we don't love ourselves, we'll love other people the wrong way. If you don't regularly give yourself compassion, kindness, and grace, you'll be a bad practitioner of it with other people. Here's the thing: We know a lot of folks say that when you don't love yourself, you don't love others. It's not really true. Girls and women are known for overextending grace, kindness, care, compassion, and adoration to everyone but ourselves. But when we love others more than we love ourselves, we have bad boundaries. When we give too much, we leave little for ourselves, and it creates nonreciprocal conditions. You give. Others take. Or conversely, you take and others give. That's bad business.

A lot of you might be saying, *OK, I hear you. But how do I do it?* Here are a few tips:

GET IN YOUR MIRROR EVERY DAY Look yourself in the eye and say, "I love you!" It sounds corny and you might not believe it at first, but you'll find it harder and harder to let that person in the mirror down by moving in unloving ways toward yourself, if you know that every day you have to look that girl in the face and confess your love. That's deep, right?

IF YOU CAN'T DO THIS MIRROR THING YET, just pick one part of your body that you love! Your eyebrows, your hair, your nails, your butt, your thighs. Anything. And love it.

PICK SOMETHING NONPHYSICAL THAT YOU LIKE ABOUT YOURSELF Are you a good friend, a good daughter, a good leader, a great poet, great at telling jokes, great at keeping other people's secrets (not the unsafe ones, mind you)? If so, then awesome! Celebrate these things about yourself.

ASK YOUR FRIENDS TO TELL YOU WHAT YOUR BEST QUALITIES ARE Or your mom. Or your nana. And then accept and receive the truth of what they say.

PRACTICE, PRACTICE, PRACTICE POINTING TO THE POSITIVE and affirming it. You'll come to see that eventually you will know what is true about you and you will love those things.

BOSSIN' UP

bôs·en əp

verb | origin: hip-hop | opposite of hierarchal, domineering, competitive

The act of directing the full capacity of your time, talents, and attention toward a specific goal, dream, or intention; owning your own power and purpose in the face of obstacles; stepping up and/or raising your standard; the pre-steps to being bossed up, slaying, or succeeding in something amazing.

Seems like everywhere we turn people are talking about being bossed up or being on their boss tip. But what does it mean for navigating girlhood as a budding feminist? Is there room for more than one boss? What if you don't really feel like a boss and you don't feel like that label fits you? And isn't bossin' the epitome of capitalist patriarchy? As feminists, we believe in a version of boss-hood that isn't rooted in materialistic gains, competition, and domination. Rather, when we boss up, we are owning our power and defining the paths for our lives, and we're doing so with confidence and swag. When feminists boss up, we are unstoppable. So, let's get into this boss shit.

WHEN YOU'RE ALREADY BOSSED UP

OK, li'l queen. We see you! You're class president, you're sitting pretty on the honor roll, you're captain of the cheerleading squad, and you started your school's Gay-Straight Alliance. You got the vote for Most Likely to Succeed in the bag and you already have a plan for the next five years. "Boss" is your middle name. Here's what you need to know to stay a boss chick:

REMEMBER WHO YOU ARE TODAY We want you to hold on to the knowledge that you are the shit, as if your life depends on it. There will be a time when someone will try to tell you otherwise. They will try to make you think you're not good enough and that you don't belong. We have found that there are so many girls who are just like you. They are smart, ambitious, and confident, with a light that shines so bright on everything they touch. Then the world takes it away. In fact, studies show that girls' confidence begins plummeting significantly at twelve years old. You may meet new challenges and self-doubt may begin to creep in. When this happens, remember who you are right now—in this moment. Write it down. Take a picture. *Just remember.* And then pull on the memories of who you are now to remind yourself, "I been on!"

TAKE RISKS Those of us who are go-getters sometimes struggle with perfectionism. If we aren't 100 percent certain we'll be good at something, we won't even try! Don't be afraid to fail. Have you ever heard the "prayer" *Lord, give me the confidence of a mediocre white boy?* That little plea is really a reflection of the way that boys take *waaay* more risks than girls. You do not have to be great at everything you do. In fact, make it a point to do something you're bad at on purpose.

SET BOUNDARIES You know another thing that happens when you're super dope? Everybody wants a piece of you! I mean, sheesh, can you breathe?! On the one hand, it may feel really good that people know you're awesome and can be trusted to get things done. On the other hand, it can also be very draining and before you know it, you're exhausted from doing things that you didn't even want to do! This is going to be a lifelong issue, but listen to your gut on this. If you're beginning to feel resentment, that's generally a sign that you're doing too much. Reevaluate and make sure this is what you want to be doing or is something that's going to move you forward. "No" can be one of the hardest words for women and girls to say, so start practicing it now. We're not saying that you shouldn't help people unless it benefits you (where's the feminism in that?). We're just saying you should make sure there's a balance and start practicing setting boundaries. (A quick heads-up: just because you say no, it doesn't mean everyone's going to respect your no. We'll let you know what to do about that once we figure it out!)

PUT YOUR PEOPLE ON Sometimes we fall for the myth that leadership is an individual thing. That there can only be one leader and that there's one kind of best. But real boss chicks find ways to help other people shine by highlighting their strengths. It's like Harry Potter and his crew. Harry was the man and all, but everybody brought different strengths to bear to get the job done. Harry's light wasn't dimmed by helping other people shine. In fact, everyone's light was brighter as a crew.

WHEN YOU'RE A REGULAR, SHMEGULAR, DEGULAR GIRL

Everybody's talking about bossin' up, but you're just chillin'. You have decent grades but you're not top of your class. You're on the yearbook committee but not the editor in chief. You play your role on the basketball team, but you're not the star player. Or maybe you were top of the class in middle school, but these advanced classes in high school have you holding down a steady C. Here's what you need to know to boss up.

BE YOUR OWN BOSS First of all, you're just fine. A lot of people believe that being a boss is about being in charge or being the best. But what's so wrong with being average? Most people in the world are average. The outliers get all the attention but they are the exception, not the rule.

Now, this does not mean that you don't have a gift. You do, and if you don't know what it is yet, that's the journey you need to take. We all have a responsibility to find our gifts and use them to the betterment of others. You may not be the next Toni Morrison, but that doesn't mean you don't have a gift for expressing your thoughts and conveying truths through the written word. Being a boss is about knowing who you are and knowing your purpose. If you're taking ownership of your life and your future and constantly pushing yourself to be better, then you're a boss. Period!

CHECK FOR IMPOSTER SYNDROME Maybe you're good where you are and you really are just chilling. But do a quick internal check and make sure that you're not holding back what you have to give for other reasons. It could be about fear of failing (see above), but it can also be imposter syndrome. Imposter syndrome is a psychological pattern that makes you doubt your accomplishments and have a fear of being exposed as a fraud, hence an "imposter." Imposter syndrome is sneaky and sometimes it shows up in the oddest places. You could be with your friends on the dance team, and all of a sudden start thinking that you made the team by accident and they are going to find out that you really can't dance and aren't nearly as good as everyone else!

DON'T COMPARE YOURSELF TO OTHERS Comparison is a tool of the devil, chile, and it'll have you out here looking a whole mess walking someone else's path. Our gardens don't grow by watching what's going on in the yard next door. Worry about yourself! We have to nurture our own gardens in order for them to grow. The only person you should be comparing yourself to is you. You have to set individual goals that have nothing to do with what other people are doing. Maybe you never place at the track meets, but is your time improving? Are you jumping higher than you did last season? Are you running longer? Stay in your lane.

WORK HARD AND STUDY YOUR CRAFT We also want you to take yourself and your gifts seriously. You have to pay the cost to be the boss. The way you do that is by putting the work into learning as much as you can about your chosen area and pushing to better yourself in that area. As J. Cole says, "I study the greats. I'm the greatest right now." So, study the greats in your craft of choice. You want to be a writer? Who were the writers who came before you? You want to be a makeup artist? Read up on the history of makeup. What were the trends thirty years ago, and how have they shifted today? You want to direct movies? Take a class on the topic. Then, in the words of Rihanna, you gotta "work, work, work, work, work, work."

It has been said that it takes about 10,000 hours to master any subject. Now, we don't know if this is exactly true, but we do know that having a serious work ethic can set many people apart from their peers. Bosses aren't born, they're made.

WHEN THEY WON'T LET YOU BE GREAT

Some of us know we're amazing, but our brilliance is never recognized. We're working hard at practice, putting in extra hours outside of the gym, and helping our teammates be better. We're better than 99 percent of the team, but during the game, we're sitting on the sidelines again. So how can you be a boss when they won't let you be great?

MAYBE YOU SHOULD GO This isn't always an option, but when it is, you should consider if you really need to be somewhere you aren't valued. We believe there are two kinds of people in the world—those who think you're dope (they think your contributions matter and see your brilliance from a mile away) and those who don't. We often spend far too much time trying to convince people we're dope when those people were never going to see it anyway. You could decide to focus your time and energy where it's valued. (Keep this little nugget in mind for dating too. Wink emoji.).

BE UNDENIABLE What sometimes happens when people aren't checking for you is you completely check out. You turn in subpar work. You're late to meetings. You don't participate in conversations. It's like, why even bother?

Here's why: Because this isn't about them. It's about you! You do good work because it's who you are. Keep your stuff so tight that they can't deny you. Be undeniably good. Either they'll have to recognize it or look like damn fools trying not to.

GET A CREW There's nothing like a good crew. See, a good crew knows your value and affirms you. It's not a superficial affirmation to make you feel good. It's really recognizing your strengths and coming to you for those things. You have to have at least one space, one person who sees your shine. Maybe it's the people at your church who call on you to lead prayer because they love how well you speak. Maybe it's your best friend, who always calls you when she's stuck on an assignment because she loves the way you break things down. Or maybe it's your English teacher, who always praises your work for being well organized and thorough. Remember these spaces when others won't let you be great.

Who are the people who believe in your greatness? Who is your crew?

BE UNBOTHERED So much about being a girl is about people devaluing you. Being a girl boss is learning to value yourself through knowledge of self. You have to know who you are and what you bring to the table. Many of us are forced to know who we are because the world screws us over so much. But when you know who you are—like, *really* know who you are—you can be in any room and sit at any table. You enter those spaces courageously. They're still going to think you're wack. But oh well. You're in the same room they're in. Ha-ha!

We love to watch the way some older Black women move through a room. They really know themselves and almost don't give a shit. (Think: Maxine Waters.) They are the embodiment of the question "Who gon' check me, boo?" They have an in-touchness with themselves and an attitude of being completely unbothered and neva scared. Get like them!

REMEMBER WHY YOU'RE THERE Sometimes we can survive hostile spaces by remembering why we're there in the first place. When Chanel would feel down in graduate school, she would listen to Jeezy singing "I do it for the hood," to remember who she was there for. Maybe you're the only Black student in an accelerated physics class and your goal is to teach STEM to kids in your community. Maybe you're the only girl on your baseball team and you want to show younger girls that baseball is cool. Or maybe you're the only feminist in Student Government Assembly and your goal is to disrupt tired male-centered notions of leadership. Whatever it is, remember why you're there. These are tough spaces to be in and it can feel like you're fighting an uphill battle. But you're not there for them anyway. You have a bigger purpose, so keep your eyes on the prize. And celebrate small wins.

A PLAYLIST
FOR FEELING

Beyoncé, "DIVA"

Iggy Azalea, "FANCY"

Rihanna, "WORK"

Alicia Keys, "GIRL ON FIRE"

Ciara, "GIRL GANG"

Destiny's Child,
"INDEPENDENT WOMEN PART I"

Gwen Stefani, "HOLLABACK GIRL"

Demi Lovato, "CONFIDENT"

Beyoncé, "SHINING"

Kelis, "BOSSY"

Remy Ma, "CONCEITED"

Beyoncé, "I BEEN ON"

Cardi B, "BODAK YELLOW"

Beyoncé, "FORMATION"

LIKE A BOSS

Santigold, "CAN'T GET ENOUGH OF MYSELF"

Nina Simone, "FEELING GOOD"

Bomba Estéreo, "SOY YO"

M.I.A., "BAD GIRLS"

Britney Spears, "WORK BITCH"

Nicki Minaj, "BEEZ IN THE TRAP"

Beyoncé, "RUN THE WORLD (GIRLS)"

Ciara, "LEVEL UP"

Nicki Minaj, Beyoncé, "FEELING MYSELF"

Lizzo, "SOULMATE"

Soulja Boy, "PRETTY BOY SWAG"

NICE FOR WHAT?

Well-Behaved Women
Seldom Make History.

–Laurel Thatcher Ulrich

WHAT ARE GIRLS MADE OF? _____

You've probably heard the rhyme that goes:

Sugar and spice

And everything nice

That's what little girls are made of

Sounds innocent enough, right? Sounds like the beginning of a delicious recipe and is certainly supposed to be a compliment. Nice means to be pleasant, amiable, delightful, and friendly. Those are all good qualities to have. What's so wrong with being nice? Well, what if we told you there's something a bit more sinister in between the lines? What if we told you that for girls, there's a subtext to being nice that is really about being compliant, obedient, and submissive?

Check it: being nice is often about appearances. Literally, "niceties" refer to the social customs we believe folks should engage in, like smiling, saying hello, holding doors open for folks, and the like. There's not necessarily anything wrong with smiling, greeting folks, or being polite. Generally, these behaviors show respect for others. But there are other times when folks want you to behave in "nice" ways that aren't really very nice. Say you're out somewhere and someone, usually a guy, tells you to smile. You're moving through the world, minding your business, and here this fool comes. You could be upset, you could be deep in thought, you could be doing quadratic equations or figuring out how to achieve world peace! But this whole other person thinks you look "prettier when you smile." It might seem like a harmless request, but in reality niceness functions as a disciplinary tool to keep women and girls in check. Uh-uh. You don't owe anyone your smile. Niceness forces girls to shrink, to not take up space, to not be loud, to be silent. The idea is that girls should go out of their way to agree with others, concede to others' points of view, and not be difficult. When we don't comply, we are called unreasonable, selfish, unfeminine—or straight-up bitches—whenever we stand up for ourselves or push back on things that aren't serving us well.

For Black girls in particular, we are not only told to be nice, we are also told that we should not be angry, lest we be seen as Angry Black Women. This is a pervasive idea that structures almost every Black woman's life. You know her. The mean Black girl with the attitude who overreacts to everything. Even Michelle Obama could not escape this trope.

When people label you as angry, the intention is to silence and discredit you. They try to convince you that your anger is illogical and that anger itself is a lesser emotion. (But no one says this about all these angry white boys running around shooting up entire schools because they've been "bullied and rejected.") But the three of us understand and treat anger as a superpower. Brittney says Black girls are masters of *eloquent rage*. Anger is a reasonable response to dealing with the foolery of racism, sexism, homophobia, transphobia, and every other thing each day of our lives. Our anger is a compass that tells us that we have been hurt in some way or experienced an injustice. The desire to be treated justly is fundamental to being human. When we are treated unjustly, we get angry—also a human response. To deny our right to our anger is to deny our right to our humanity.

But we call anger a superpower because being mad doesn't mean you have to tear things down and eff things up. When you get mad, first, make sure you are clear about what has offended you or done you harm. Next step: get to building the world you want to see. (You might wanna process it with one of your people first. Don't keep all that negative energy in! And then get back to building.) Given that we will always have endless wells of rage until the revolution comes, this also means we'll have endless wells of power to build toward a different future. That's a superpower!

We are part of an entire legacy of women who pushed for change because they were mad as hell. Ida B. Wells was mad as hell when her friend was lynched by a white mob—so mad that she made it her life's work to report on the vicious violence against African Americans in the Jim Crow South. When Grace Lee Boggs dedicated her life to fighting against the injustices faced by Black people, women, and the working class, do you think she cared whether people thought of her as nice? Dolores Huerta was fed up when she left her teaching job to organize for farm workers' rights, later saying, "I couldn't tolerate seeing kids come to class hungry and needing shoes. I thought I could do more by organizing farm workers than by trying to teach their hungry children." And when Alicia Garza, Opal Tometi, and Patrisse Cullors started the hashtag #BlackLivesMatter, they were mad AF that seventeen-year-old Trayvon Martin had been murdered and his murderer had been acquitted. They were angry that the lives of Black people, even Black children, seemed so disposable.

This is why they'd rather us be nice. Nice girls don't make the kind of trouble that leads to real institutional and cultural change. Forget being nice. You deserve to take up space and speak your mind. Make a little trouble, girl.

Plus, have you noticed the messages that boys get? They are told to speak up, make noise, be assertive, and act as leaders. They aren't told to smile more, be pleasant, or consider other people's feelings. Now, we could all benefit from considering others' feelings and taking other people's points of view into consideration. And there's nothing wrong with smiling—if you feel like it! But society focuses on preparing boys to be leaders while girls have to fall in line, and being nice is part of that indoctrination. That shit is for the birds.

SOME WORDS OF ADVICE

BE KIND, NOT NICE Now, to be clear, we are not telling you to be mean or unkind. There's a difference between being nice and being kind. Rejecting that fake niceness is not a hall pass to be a mean girl. It is important to respect others—their boundaries and their process. That's also part of being kind.

Being kind is about being caring and compassionate. It's about empathizing with others. Being kind means checking your privilege. Being kind does not mean shrinking yourself to fit others' labels or expectations. Being kind is about being a member of your community who fights for justice and is accountable to others. Above all, being kind does not mean playing small. Because what does playing small get you?

You already know the answer.

DON'T SHRINK Sometimes being nice is about not taking up too much room or being the center of attention. Now, no one likes an attention hog, but there's a difference between being obnoxious and being confident. You don't have to make yourself small to make others comfortable. A friend, family member—anyone—who feels like your light must be dimmed so they can shine is a straight-up hater. Period. We all can win. Don't shrink yourself to fit someone else's definition of what a girl or young person should be. We're not saying this is going to be easy. It is hard to unlearn everything you've been taught about what it means to be a girl. You may feel a twinge when you say no or attempt to set boundaries. You may feel like you are being mean. Back your guilt down! Say no anyway.

NO IS A COMPLETE SENTENCE Having boundaries is an important aspect of not only folks respecting you, but of you respecting yourself. If you don't want to go somewhere, you don't have to be "nice" and go to that place because your sibling/homie/bae wants you to go. You can say no. No is a complete sentence. If you don't want to engage in certain behavior, you don't have to. That is a boundary you can set for yourself. And it is, in fact, not nice to yourself to twist and bend to please others at the expense of your own desires.

Abusers who prey on girls often count on niceness to work in their favor. Because so many girls are raised to be nice—to be obedient, to comply, to put others' needs in front of their own—some abusers use this to groom their victims. These abusers understand that girls are usually taught to honor other people's wishes more than their own boundaries and use this fact against those who are most vulnerable. Abusers may weaponize your niceness against you. This is not your fault, and we aren't blaming you. Forewarned, as the saying goes, is forearmed. They may try to get you to believe it is "nice" to allow them to treat you with disrespect, have access to your body, or to treat you in other ways that you don't like. If you or a girl you know is experiencing this sort of boundary crossing, tell an adult you trust—even if the person violating your trust is a family member, teacher, or another young person close to you. Being nice does not mean that you have to consent to any and everything.

WARNING! BUT LET'S KEEP IT REAL There are social repercussions and personal repercussions to not being "nice." When you defy society's expectations of how girls should behave, some folks might feel some type of way. They might tell you that you're being bitchy, that you're mean, that you're . . . not nice. Folks might confront you, try to bully you. There are also extreme reactions to girls and women asserting boundaries. Some have been attacked or worse for saying no.

Think about a moment when you were uncomfortable but you didn't speak up. Why didn't you? Did you feel scared of how others might react? That's a perfectly normal feeling, because there are so many opinions on how girls and women should behave. Maybe you've noticed the women in your life being really "nice" even when they don't want be? They might be being nice because, like you, they are afraid of the consequences of not being nice. The truth is, being "nice" in certain circumstances—like with a sexist boss, a catcaller, an ex—can be a strategy that girls and women use to survive. Still, recognizing niceness as a way to move through the world when you don't have a lot of options doesn't mean you owe it to anyone. It can be part of your toolkit you use to make it through the day, but this says more about the effed-up world we live in than who you are as a person—'cause we already know you're dope.

BOOKS/ESSAYS TO CHECK OUT THAT HELP YOU *STOP BEING SO NICE*

ELOQUENT RAGE **by Brittney Cooper**

DIFFICULT WOMEN **by Roxane Gay**

GOOD AND MAD: THE REVOLUTIONARY POWER OF WOMEN'S ANGER **by Rebecca Traister**

RAGE BECOMES HER: THE POWER OF WOMEN'S ANGER **by Soraya Chemaly**

"THE USES OF ANGER," IN SISTER OUTSIDER **by Audre Lorde**

CAN WE LIVE?

COME CELEBRATE
WITH ME THAT EVERYDAY
SOMETHING HAS TRIED TO KILL ME
AND HAS FAILED.

—Lucille Clifton

As women of color, we go through a lot! So when we make it through, we wear our resiliency as a badge of honor. When people say we are strong sisters, we hold our heads up higher. We are celebrated for our abilities to push back pain and keep it moving. Our ability to respond to life's hardships by portraying strength and hiding our trauma becomes the measure by which we define our womanhood. And with so many negative stereotypes circulating about us being angry, loud, ghetto, lazy, and so on, who can blame us for wanting to relish the seemingly positive idea that we are strong and we are built for this? We feel like Mama Clifton said: ". . . come celebrate / with me that everyday / something has tried to kill me / and has failed."

But we're here to tell you that our resiliency is a trap and is rooted in white-supremacist patriarchy. The lie white supremacy tells us is that Black people are preternaturally strong, like superhero levels of strong.

Since Black women were first brought to this country, we have been asked to be strong. One of the most offensive slavery myths was that Africans were more suited to hot weather and that they were genetically predestined to work on plantations. Our strength was supposedly so magical that even Black children as young as six were able to do the same work as adults because they were not as fragile as white children. For Black women who were enslaved, our assumed supernatural strength created expectations that we could give birth and return to the gruesome work of the fields within days. Sis, it takes weeks, sometimes even months, to recover from childbirth! We are just over 150 years removed from slavery—we've been free for less time than we were enslaved—and some of these narratives still show up to shape our story.

WHY IT MATTERS

The other reason why resiliency is a trap is because the idea that we are so strong makes it hard for other people to see us as victims, even when terrible things happen to us. And we do not get the same outrage as the boys who are victims of injustice.

Black girls are constantly the victims of vicious violence, and it often feels like no one is fighting for us. Take the 1992 murder of fifteen-year-old Latasha Harlins, for example. Latasha Harlins was shot in the back of the head by a Korean American convenience-store cashier who accused her of attempting to steal a $1.79 bottle of orange juice, even though she had the money in her hand. To make matters worse, the convenience-store cashier avoided any jail time when the judge went against the jury recommendation of sixteen years in prison. The judge determined that, while she thought the cashier acted "inappropriately," the "reaction was understandable." Although this was one of the sparks that led to the 1992 L.A. riots, it wasn't until the brutal beating of a Black man, Rodney King, that the city erupted in protest. Today, Latasha is barely a footnote in the story, and while King's case resulted in policy changes and changes in policing, no such changes happened as a result of the murder of Latasha.

These stories still happen today. For example, in 2015 in McKinney, Texas, a fifteen-year-old-girl, leaving a pool party in a bikini, was grabbed by the back of her head, forced to the ground facedown, and pinned there by a police officer. When other teens tried to come to her defense, he drew guns on them while the girl cried out for her mother. That same year, we watched in horror as cell-phone footage captured a police officer at a high school in South Carolina body-slamming a young Black girl and dragging her frail body across the classroom. In 2021, on the same day we were exhaling a collective sigh of relief knowing that there would be accountability for the officer who took George Floyd's life, sixteen-year-old Ma'Khia Bryant was fatally shot by a police officer in Columbus, Ohio, when she called 911 for help. While these videos are just as horrific as those that showcase the violence against Black boys, they don't spark the same level of national outrage.

And it's not just other races we have to worry about; we are victims of violence within our own communities. And we're not even talking about sexual assault—there are countless stories of Black girls being physically beaten by Black boys. In March 2020, we were appalled by the video of a fifteen-year-old young Black girl in Brooklyn being jumped by over a dozen Black boys, kicking her in the chest and face and stealing her Jordans. Queer Black girls are also attacked and are punished more for living in their truth. In 2003, fifteen-year-old Sakia Gunn was killed by a twenty-eight-year-old Black man who tried to holler at her. She told him she was a lesbian and he killed her. In 2015, twenty-one-year-old Zella Ziona, living her life as a trans girl with family and friends who loved her, was killed by her cis "friend" she had known since high school. He was apparently upset because she had flirted with him in front of his friends, and he retaliated by shooting her in an alley, in the head and in the groin. In 2020, high school student Brayla Stone, a seventeen-year-old trans Black girl, was run down by a car in a targeted act of violence. There have been no marches for Sakia, Zella, or Brayla.

Even when we are not the direct victims of violence, we often bear witness to some of the most horrific instances in our people's history. Trayvon Martin was on the phone with his friend Rachel Jeantel when he was followed and murdered by an overzealous neighborhood watchman. When Rachel testified on his behalf, she was ridiculed for her demeanor, how she spoke, and even called a "train wreck." Not only did she have to hear her best friend being murdered, she had to bear the brunt of being blamed for the acquittal of his murderer. When that young girl in South Carolina was being attacked, it was Niya Kenny, another Black girl in her class, who stood up and said, "You can't do this! Someone needs to record this!" How was she rewarded? She was suspended from school for being a disruption. (When her mother was interviewed, she rightly called out the police for being the true disruption in the classroom). And it was seventeen-year-old Darnella Frazier who filmed the murder of George Floyd, which resulted in charges against the officers and sparked a worldwide movement. But instead of just being celebrated as a brave citizen journalist, she was criticized for not having done enough and accused of recording the video for clout. Do we ever stop to wonder about the price of bearing witness and the extra burden that comes with being criticized for not doing enough? Bearing witness requires a certain kind of strength. And Black girls are not only asked to grin and bear it, they are often scrutinized when they do so.

Then the very things we do for our own survival and the survival of our people further reinforce stereotypes about who we are as Black girls and women. Our strength and ability to survive really inhumane conditions become the standard for other Black women and girls to live up to. The fact that we stand tall out of necessity becomes the very thing that defines us. It become "Black girls don't cry. That's that white-girl mess." Even in the face of street harassment, sexual assault, physical violence, failing schools, ICE raids, deportation of family members, mental instability, police brutality, and more. It's an all-encompassing web that we spend our entire lives trying to unweave.

Part of resisting the lies white supremacy tells us is resisting the idea that we always have to be strong. Here's the thing: you are strong and dope and resilient. However, there can be too much of a good thing. The pressure to be perfect, to hold it all together, to never lose your cool can be incredibly damaging. And the effect of stress on our bodies ain't no joke. Your body can't tell the difference between the stress from trying to be strong or from running from a tiger. The stress hormones are the same. Your heart races, your breath gets faster, and your muscles tense up. In addition to mental anguish, stress can lead to high blood pressure, headaches, missed periods, stomachaches, heart disease, diabetes, and so much more. Being strong is killing us.

We'd much rather you be

free. Part of being free is being able to show up as full humans who love, hurt, get overwhelmed, have joys and fears, and who can see when they are not OK. What would happen if you relieved yourself of the mandate to be strong all the time and allowed the tears to fall a little? Down with the superwoman—you are enough and you are magic.

We don't have many tips to offer you in this chapter, because to keep it real with you, we still have not figured this resiliency thing all the way out ourselves. We still struggle with how we define ourselves in a world determined to define us. You are not alone. So we share our own stories about how resiliency showed up for us during our girlhood so that you know that we—like most women of color—have been exactly where you are. We're going to get free together.

OUR STORIES

Susana's Story

At my fifth-grade graduation we all received special awards for attending an afterschool program. Our principal stood at the podium and read out superlatives about each student as she handed out a painted a figurine with a burgundy cap and gown. She'd say, "Dante is a special kid because he's a great speller" or "Julissa is a special kid because she got an A in math all year." Stuff like that. I waited with a whole lot of anticipation to hear my name called. As a young girl, I soaked up praise like a sponge. There could never be too much. My principal started describing the next recipient and I started feeling hype! By the description I just knew it was me. She said, "This young lady is incredibly bright. She's a classroom leader who's not afraid to speak her mind. I just know she's going to grow up to be a lawyer and fight for justice!" Folks started clapping loud. My cheeks were flushed with pride. I wanted to grow up to be a teacher but, shoot, I'd be a lawyer!

Then she spoke a name that was not my own. My bestie stood up, smiled, and strutted to the podium to get her award. My face burned with shame and embarrassment. The girl the principal described was me, couldn't everybody see that?

Looking back, though, my principal judged the best she could. Yes, I was a smart girl who spoke in class and had opinions. But mostly, I was a quiet rule follower who tried to stay out of trouble. I was not in class acting like a future Justice Sonia Sotomayor. See, I had learned early on to keep my head down and my mouth shut. I hated getting in trouble or having adults mad at me. That happens sometimes when kids experience bullying, abuse, or neglect early on in life. You try to navigate a scary world by making yourself small, not causing a scene, grateful to make it through a day without someone berating or violating you.

Resilience isn't always putting your hands on your hips and staring down the bully. Sometimes it's just surviving to live another day. That was how I felt. That's certainly how I acted. Resiliency meant that I was shrinking myself and making myself smaller. But deep down, I had lots of feelings and opinions. I wanted to live my life out loud but was terrified of being ridiculed or getting in trouble.

When my principal finally described me, her voice was soft and mild: "This young lady is so sweet and well mannered. She does all her work and is very kind." At the time, that description sounded wack as hell, but instead of cutting up, I swallowed my disappointment, strode to the podium, took my award, and sat down with a smile.

Brittney's Story

When I was in sixth grade, I struggled with thoughts of suicide. Two years before, I had lost my dad to gun violence, and I never even missed a day of school! I was proud of myself at the time, because I thought that this was what it meant to be strong. I thought this was what it meant to be a good daughter to a hardworking single mother. I didn't want to cause any problems with all my feelings. I particularly loved it when my Girl Scout troop painted me a banner that said WE LOVE YOU, BRIT (they ran out of space on the paper for the rest of my name!) and drove it over to my house after the meeting. (Crew is necessary, like we said.)

But looking back, I don't recommend keeping it all in. In sixth grade, the unprocessed grief showed up. I also had a teacher who humiliated me in math class every day and tried to kill my confidence. For part of each day, I took gifted courses, and we learned some of the math before we did it in my actual math class. But my teacher seemed to be very bothered by a confident Black girl daring to take up space and answer all the questions right (#BlackGirlMagic!). So by the end of every class, I would be lying head down on my desk, crying. I didn't want to tell my mom because I thought maybe I had done something wrong.

And then there was the day when I spaced out and cut the line at the water fountain. It was a messed-up thing to do, but I honestly was so zoned out thinking about something else that I didn't realize another kid, a white boy, was waiting. Angry at me, he called me "nigger" under his breath. But I heard it, and yelled, "A nigger is an ignorant person!" My teacher, a Black woman, sent us both to the office, him for using the word, and me for using that word in my retort. I had never been sent to the office, and I knew it was unjust when he was the one using racially offensive terms. The kid's mom taught at our school, and maybe our Black principal wasn't comfortable disciplining him. Whatever the reason, when you're a Black girl, the gaslighting and denial of your feelings and experiences starts early. What it meant for my grieving self and my fragile mental health was that I had lots of rage and sadness and no proper outlets to express it.

Seemingly out of nowhere, I became obsessed with death and dying and spent a lot of time thinking of ways to kill myself. It really didn't come out of nowhere. I was in a stressful school environment every day, with the pressure to make good grades and navigate racist teachers and students. Plus I was dealing with the trauma of losing a parent to violence. It really sucked.

I struggled for two years before I finally asked my mom for help. Thankfully, she took me to a therapist, but if I had gone sooner, maybe I wouldn't have felt so bad for so long.

Chanel's Story

When I was eleven years old, my mother died. One day, my father sat me down to tell me that she was dying and two weeks later she was gone. It was difficult to carry on with my life with such a gaping hole in my heart, but somewhere along the way I decided that I hated sympathy and I never wanted anyone to see me cry. So I kept it all inside until I could come home to a private space. When I graduated high school, I was featured in the newspaper and spoke about my mother's death. There were so many people who had been my friends since middle school who had no idea that my mother died because I purposefully never told them. I also didn't share my sad days with my family because I didn't want to trigger their pain around losing my mother. I was more concerned with other people's reactions than my own needs. And therapy wasn't even a blip on my radar.

I learned to internalize stress and was really good at putting my emotional needs to the side. I found escapes. I kept myself busy, studied a lot, and maintained a great social life. I was so good at compartmentalizing that I could schedule my tears! But holding all that in was not good for me.

It meant that people would unload so much emotional baggage on me, because they had no idea what I was going through. It meant that I would put my feelings aside for other people's, and I had no place to go either. Eventually, holding my pain and the burdens of other people broke me physically and mentally, and I had to do a lot of work to heal myself. I had to learn to be vulnerable and share when I'm not OK, especially with the people who love me the most.

#BlackGirlMagic

Audre Lorde told us that "we were never meant to survive." Yet here we are. This is what CaShawn Thompson was referring to when she started using the phrase #BlackGirlMagic on Twitter in 2015. She created a gorgeous way of capturing all the things Black girls and women go through and overcome in a world filled with white supremacy, patriarchy, and capitalist excess.

Part of the reason we have to celebrate the particular magic of Black girls and women is because so much of society is built on the idea that we are too much of the wrong thing and too little of the right thing. We are called too loud, too fast, too fat, too fertile, too angry, too Black, too uncouth, too everything. Meanwhile, these same folks don't recognize how smart we are, how loving, how beautiful, and how much creativity and ingenuity we possess. Black-girl magic is a celebration of the ways we have turned our pain into passion, power, and purpose. 'Cause you know what? The struggle is real. But the magic is too. We need to celebrate our magic while also making space for our struggle.

QUOTES TO
MEMORIZE

"CARING FOR MYSELF IS NOT SELF-INDULGENCE, IT IS
SELF-PRESERVATION, AND THAT IS AN ACT OF POLITICAL
WARFARE."
–Audre Lorde, *A Burst of Light and Other Essays*

"IF I DIDN'T DEFINE MYSELF FOR MYSELF, I WOULD BE CRUNCHED
INTO OTHER PEOPLE'S FANTASIES FOR ME AND EATEN ALIVE."
–Audre Lorde, speech at Harvard University, 1982

"YOU WANNA FLY, YOU GOTTA GIVE UP THE SHIT THAT WEIGHS
YOU DOWN."
–Toni Morrison, *Song of Solomon*

RESOURCES TO CHECK OUT

Podcast: *Therapy for Black Girls*

Instagram: Sad Girls Club

App: Shine

Website: thisisdrkbeauty.com

Organization: GirlTrek

Books, Essays, and Poems:

Black Macho and the Myth of the Superwoman by Michele Wallace

"A Litany for Survival" by Audre Lorde

"How to Not Die" by Robin Boylorn/Crunk Feminist Collective

In Search of Our Mothers' Gardens by Alice Walker

Wild Seed by Octavia Butler

BLACK GIRL MAGIC PRO TIP

Find at least one space to be vulnerable. Someone you can be soft with. Where is that place for you and who is that person? You should also be that space for others. Have y'all seen those memes that say "Check on your strong friend"? That's the kind of friendship we're talking about. Let your friends know they don't have to be strong with you. That you see their humanity and are asking, "Sis, how are you? No, really? How are you? I know you said you're fine. But are you well? Do you feel mentally tough and ready to conquer all, or are you struggling?" Think of that Destiny's Child video "Girl," where Beyoncé and Michelle had to sit Kelly down and let her know that they see her hurting and want to check on her. Normalize holding your friends accountable to being vulnerable in your presence. To some people, our tears may not hold the same weight as "white-girl tears," but they do matter. We need somewhere where we can go and be seen—our pain and our joy.

SEXUAL ASSAULT

We live in a culture that fails Black girls through the perpetuation of the idea that sexual violence done to our bodies is either normal, impossible, unimportant, or our own fault. One in nine girls in the United States has experienced sexual assault at the hands of an adult, and 47 percent of trans people have been sexually assaulted in their lifetime. It is an epidemic for Black and Brown girls, yet there are no news stories, no community outrage, no petitions signed.

Can "somebody/anybody sing a Black girl's song"?

And it is by the people we call our own in the places we call home that we are made aware of the downside of what it means to be a Black girl. For cis girls and trans girls alike, it is cis Black men who are most likely to be at the root of our violence. When we experience bodily harm, at the hands of men, some of whom we know, it becomes clear why we need intersectional feminism. Our Combahee River Collective foremothers told us "we struggle together with Black men against racism, while we also struggle with Black men about sexism." We remember Toyin Salau, who marched for Black Lives only to be raped and murdered by a Black man days later.

Can "somebody/anybody sing a Black girl's song"?

We live in a state of sexual violence that is so common that we can all sing along to it. We call this rape culture: the everyday cultural practices that make sexual violence seem normal and uphold the idea that men determine consent. We move our shoulders while singing, "I hate these blurred lines, I know you want it." We shout in unison at the club, "Put Molly all in her Champagne, she ain't even know it. I took her home and enjoyed that, she ain't even know it." We rock our hips while they tell us how they'll beat it up, hit it, bust it open, kill it. Sexual violence is a bop! We are entertained by it, eating popcorn while watching the fifty-plus rape scenes on *Game of Thrones*. Buying tickets to root for a hundred-year-old vampire to finally land the seventeen-year-old girl of his dreams. #RelationshipGoals. It's sold to us for $9.99 in magazine ads with women tied up, gagged, and surrounded by groups of shirtless men. Sexual assault is edgy and artistic.

It is at our dinner tables when a celebrity is accused of sexual assault and we immediately talk about the woman as a gold-digger or wonder, "Why would he have to rape her? He can have anyone he wants." It is in the hallways at school when boys take bets about touching our bodies and on the playground when they grab our butts or play "hide and go get it." It is on the walk to the library when we are catcalled and blamed if we don't respond appropriately. It is on posters on campus teaching women how to take measures to prevent rape but not telling men they should not rape.

But can "somebody/anybody sing a Black girl's song"?

Rape culture is ugly. It ostracizes the victim by carving her into a caricature and branding her one of those fast-tail girls if she has any interest in boys or sex, or if her body has developed "too quickly." And if she dares to like it, people claim she deserves whatever happens to her. She doesn't get to experience sexuality as simply a normal part of life. Her desire is wrong. She is too much, so we throw her away. So we can protect our boys and our men. *She* made them chase her home from school, threatening to rape her. *She* made that grown man rub on her leg. *She* made those boys rip her shirt off at that party. *She* made her uncle desire her. Her supposed faults are hypervisible. The violence done to her—invisible. Grown women whisper when she walks by, roll their eyes in disdain, and hold their boyfriends' hands tighter. They protect him instead of her.

Can "somebody/anybody sing a Black girl's song?" We can and we will.

Dear Black Girl,

We want you to know our collective legacy is more than trauma and pain. All around you, past and present, there are Black women who see you and believe you. When nobody else rides for us, we ride for ourselves. We know we are worthy of saving, so we save ourselves. We sing Black-girl songs.

We sing like Tarana Burke, who started #MeToo after a thirteen-year-old girl confided in her that she had been sexually assaulted and Burke did not know how to respond. Later, she said she wished she had simply told the girl: "Me too." So she created an entire movement that made the space for the empathy that Black women and girls need.

We sing like Rosa Parks, who cut her teeth organizing as a sexual-assault investigator. Before she got on that bus, she worked for the NAACP and was called to investigate the sexual assault of a twenty-four-year-old sharecropper named Recy Taylor, who was raped by a group of white men on her way home from church. Before that, she fought off a white neighbor who tried to sexually assault her.

We sing like dream hampton, whose *Surviving R. Kelly* documentary was so powerful that a month after its release and more than twenty years after speculation that Kelly had married singer Aaliyah when he was twenty-seven and she was fifteen, he was finally charged for some of his crimes against other girls. We sing our own songs. We all we got.

Wrong is not your name. You have the right to your body. Anyone who disrespects your boundaries is wrong. Anyone who does not believe you is wrong. You are not wrong. There is nothing wrong with you. You did not do anything wrong. While we cannot fix it for you, we see you. We believe you. And we affirm and honor your truth. "Wrong," as poet and feminist June Jordan has said, "is not your name."

I AM NOT WRONG: WRONG IS NOT MY NAME
MY NAME IS MY OWN MY OWN MY OWN

–June Jordan, "Poem about My Rights"

We see you. We got you. Wrong is not your name. It's too much for any one of us to hold. Come, let us hold this together.

2
BEAUTY

DON'T TOUCH MY HAIR

Maybe you've heard the expression that a woman's hair is her crowning glory? Hair is one of many ways we can express ourselves. We can grow it long, cut it short, dye it purple, or wrap it all up in a scarf. How we choose to wear our hair is both a personal and political choice, especially for girls and particularly for girls of color.

Unfortunately, we all get judged on our looks, and hair is a big part of that. Hair reflects the real and ideal. Many folks think that long, flowing blond locks are a beauty ideal. But what if that's not what your hair looks like? You may get judged for not measuring up to this ideal that you didn't create and may not even agree with.

Hair is often one of the cues we look at to figure out a person's gender in our society, and the rules about what is appropriate shift and change with time. Look back at the paintings of the men who wrote the U.S. Constitution. Many of them rocked bumped curls and even wigs. Fast-forward to today and a cis-het man wearing a wig would likely raise a few eyebrows because of homophobic notions of masculinity. Certain hairstyles have racist and classist connotations too. When Kim Kardashian wore "boxer braids," beauty magazines called her chic, but young girls of color with cornrows have been suspended from school for wearing "distracting" and "ghetto" hairstyles. This is a double standard that can hit close to home.

A recent H&M ad caught some attention because of one model's hair. The model, a young Black girl, is seen wearing a variety of sporty outfits. Like the other kids in the ad campaign, she's supposed to represent kids at play. All the models have messy hair and joyful expressions, like they just left the playground after an afternoon of wilding out on slides, swings, and jungle gyms. The model in question has gorgeous dark-brown skin and a shy smile. Her coily hair is pulled back into a short afro puff, her edges are unlaid. A firestorm of comments flooded social media, with many commentators attacking H&M, who have previously been caught out there with racist designs, for showing a Black girl as "unkempt." The thing is, there was another Black girl who also modeled in the campaign. The difference was that she had looser curls, longer hair, and lighter skin to boot. There didn't seem to be any issue with that little girl's hair. So what was it about the first model that sparked such backlash? Could it be there is only so much space for little girls, particularly those with darker skin and tightly coiled hair, to be "messy"? If her edges had been "laid," would folks have taken issue? What should've been a dope moment to celebrate became a moment that was picked apart and scrutinized in super-negative ways.

Young women's hair is frequently discussed. It seemed like award-winning gymnast Gabby Douglas got more attention for her messy bun than her backflips during the 2012 Olympics. Many called her out for her hair, when the focus should've been on her skill on the balance beam. Blue Ivy Carter was frequently scrutinized as a baby when she sported an afro or afro puffs. Folks complained that her mother, Queen Bey herself, was not taking care of Blue's hair because she wasn't sporting laid edges or a headful of baubles and barrettes. But we don't even have to go to celebrities or athletes. Maybe you've experienced a version of this at a family dinner or at a holiday party. That auntie or uncle you only see once a year who always wants to comment on how tall you're getting or how much you've grown is all in your business talking about "What's going on with that hair?" That kind of attention can be hella embarrassing, or even angering.

Susana's Story

Let me take you through my hair journey. I got my hair relaxed when I was twelve years old. I had been begging my mama for a more "grown-up" style for a while, but she wasn't feeling it for the longest. I really wanted hair that I could flip over my shoulder and bangs I could curl with a curling iron. I wanted my hair to look like my friends' hair. When she finally said yes, I was so excited. I got to the salon and sat in the chair, burning with excitement. Then I was just burning. The stinky, noxious-smelling goop on my head that was turning my hair from curly to straight had my scalp on fire. I gritted my teeth and said it was burning, but the hairdresser told me the longer it stayed on, the straighter it would be. So I sat there feeling so damn miserable. After what seemed like an eternity, the hairdresser brought me to the sink. When the warm water hit my scalp it felt sore and tender. I was beginning to wonder if it was all worth it. But not long after getting blow dried and all curled up, I felt like it totally was. When she spun me around and I saw myself in the mirror, I saw the me I had always wanted to be. The girl in the mirror was a young woman with long, flowing hair. I looked and felt beautiful. And on the ride home, I rolled down the window of the car and let the wind blow through my hair. I felt amazing.

Unfortunately for me, that feeling didn't last long. The relaxer broke my hair off badly. For someone who really wanted long hair, seeing it get shorter and shorter was the worst. Plus, I hated going to get my hair done and dealing with a burnt scalp.

It wasn't all bad though. I would go to a girl who lived around the corner from me who did braids. She'd hook me up with box braids that swung down my back and gave me the illusion of long, thick hair. Plus it was fun to switch it up and rock different hairstyles. For my senior picture, I got a weave that gave me shoulder-length hair and a swoop bang—you really couldn't tell me nothing. Even while I worried about my "real" hair, wearing different braids and weaves reminded me that hair could be playful and fun.

Super-short bobs were all the rage when I got to college, and I rocked short cuts for a while. Even though I still longed for flowing hair, I recognized how the bob style drew attention to my face, which I was just starting to appreciate as unique and beautiful.

Still, getting my hair relaxed was a complete pain in the ass, and I totally resented all the time I spent curling and styling my hair and protecting it from the dang rain! When I turned nineteen, I was tired of the hair salon and all the foolishness. Finally I was done spending hours in the salon keeping up on styles. I had tried to grow my hair out but it was super damaged. I hated feeling judged by hair stylists who I felt were basing my worth on the quality of my hair. So I went to my hairdresser and I told her to cut it all. Her eyes widened and she was like, "Are you sure?" I nodded and her scissors went flying, clumps of dry, damaged hair floating to the ground. When she turned me around in the chair, I saw my round face framed by a halo of very short, soft, dark-brown curls. I was excited for this new 'do but also scared.

That moment in the salon marked a shift. For years, everything around me had screamed that I didn't have "good" hair, and here I was with my hair as it naturally grew out of my head. Even though I still struggled with accepting myself and my hair, I was determined to shift my perspective.

It wasn't easy at first. I remember several folks telling me I looked "like a man" and my mother questioning if I was a lesbian. My own internalized transphobia and homophobia bristled at these accusations, but over time I was able to respond by checking the haters, clapping back at their ish, and own my look. I realized: Who was anybody to comment on my looks, whether it was my clothing, my body, or my hair?! After a while, I was able to cut someone down to size with a side eye before they even moved their mouth to issue anything other than a compliment.

Although I've never relaxed my hair again, I've worn my hair a ton of ways. I've rocked afro puffs, twists, braids, locs—you name it. Thankfully hair has become mostly just another fun way to express myself.

As a Black woman, I recognize hair as political and personal. You may have already experienced this duality in your own life. Maybe you rock a hijab and folks are always in your business about what is "up under there." Or maybe you rock a baldie and folks question your choice to be hair-free. Maybe you rock waist-length hair and folks question if it's "yours." Or maybe you came to school with Bantu knots and your classmate reached out to touch your 'do without permission.

Your hair and how you decide to wear it is your choice, and there is no wrong way to do it.

#HAIRGOALS
PLAYLIST

Solange, "DON'T TOUCH MY HAIR"

India.Arie, "I AM NOT MY HAIR"

Willow Smith, "WHIP MY HAIR"

Corinne Bailey Rae, "PUT YOUR RECORDS ON"

Lady Gaga, "HAIR"

ROCK YOUR BODY, BODY

> I AM A FEMINIST, AND WHAT THAT MEANS TO ME IS MUCH THE SAME AS THE MEANING OF THE FACT THAT I AM BLACK: IT MEANS THAT I MUST UNDERTAKE TO LOVE MYSELF AND TO RESPECT MYSELF AS THOUGH MY VERY LIFE DEPENDS UPON SELF-LOVE AND SELF-RESPECT.
>
> —June Jordan, "Where Is the Love?"

This is for the girls who are never the recipients of Woman Crush Wednesday. The girls who never grace the covers of beauty magazines. The girls who are the "before" picture to someone else's "after." The girls who never see themselves reflected back in the images of Prettiest Woman in the World. This is for the girls who feel invisible.

Or maybe you're not one of these girls. Maybe you actually do fit into the ideal images of beauty, but these girls are your sisters and your friends. You want them to know that you see them even when the world doesn't. This is for you too.

Invisibility is a tricky thing. On the one hand, it's a really cool superpower. Remember how Miles Morales, aka Spider-Man, could camouflage himself, clothes and all, to match his surroundings, making him effectively invisible? Gekko from *PJ Masks* uses a secret technique to manipulate his skin tissue with primary colors to make him blend in with the environment, disappearing him from sight. And who could forget Harry Potter and that dope invisibility cloak that allowed him and his crew to secretly dash around Hogwarts unnoticed? This invisibility gave them both power and protection.

But there's a difference between *choosing* invisibility and being *made* invisible. When people are praised for losing weight and making themselves smaller, big girls are made invisible. When we see people with physical disabilities on TV only when they are overcoming a huge obstacle, that makes the everyday lives of disabled girls invisible. When we feature only cis girls when we say #BlackGirlMagic, that makes trans girls invisible. When we make healthy girls the symbol of youth and vibrancy, that makes chronically ill girls invisible. When we put forward a rigid idea of what it means to have a "good" body, we make all kinds of other bodies invisible.

And as the age-old feminist adage reminds us, the personal is political. Our bodies are often the focal points of all kinds of regulations and legislation. They dictate how we show up in the healthcare system, the education we receive, the opportunities we are given and denied, and how people perceive our capabilities. Our bodies absolutely matter. And girls who love their own bodies become women who advocate for all bodies later.

How are we going to crush girlhood if we don't love our bodies while we're doing the work?! We can't have a feminism that does not encourage all girls to love their bodies!

And we come into the world already loving our bodies. Here's how author and activist Sonya Renee Taylor puts it in her book *The Body Is Not An Apology*:

> *We did not start life in a negative partnership with our bodies. I have never seen a toddler lament the size of their thighs, the squishiness of their bellies. Children do not arrive here ashamed of their race, gender, age, or disabilities. Babies love their bodies! Each discovery they encounter is freaking awesome. Have you ever seen an infant realize they have feet? Talk about wonder! That is what an unobstructed relationship with our bodies looks like. You were an infant once, which means there was a time when you thought your body was freaking awesome too.*

So we already knew how to love our bodies. We just forgot how. Together we can remember. We want you to know we see you.

BIG GIRL . . .

We see you. We know you're asking:

How do I love this body that, in its very being, takes up too much space? How do I find a way to love myself when girls my size are never reflected as a beautiful being on TV and in magazines? When they give free T-shirts out at school, I don't even stand in line anymore. Why bother, when they never have my size in the first place? Tell me how I'm supposed to love me when I can't even eat in peace. I get an ice-cream cone and all of a sudden every damn body, including strangers I don't know from a can of paint, are soooo concerned with my health. Meanwhile, my skinny best friend just ate four slices of pizza and drank two sodas and no one batted an eye. How am I supposed to love myself when I am the butt of jokes because of my size? When the world defines my body shape as part of an epidemic? When I can't move through life without the world insisting I be smaller? How can I love a body that is invisible?

We're not going to pretend to know the answer to this. This is going to be a lifelong process between you and your body. But what we do know, unequivocally, is that your body is a gift. When you love your body, rolls and all, you teach each and every one of us that our worth is not defined by our weight. That our value to this world can't be measured by something as silly as a scale. Some girls who are small today may be big a few years from now. Bodies change; that's what they do. And when you love your big body, you open up a space for all women to love themselves if and when they are blessed with more curves. When you love your body, you teach us that *we* decide we are beautiful! And that we are wassup at any size!

YOUR ANTHEM Diamond K, "Watch Out for the Big Girl"

Words to Live By

"People always ask me, 'You have so much confidence. Where did that come from?' It came from me. One day I decided that I was beautiful, and so I carried out my life as if I was a beautiful girl . . . It doesn't have anything to do with how the world perceives you. What matters is what you see." —*Gabourey Sidibe, actor/author*

"Back when I was modeling, the first time I went to Italy I was having cappuccinos every day, and I gained like fifteen pounds. And I felt gorgeous! I would take my clothes off in front of the mirror and be like, Oh, I look like a woman. *And I felt beautiful, and I never tried to lose it, 'cause I loved it."* —*Christina Hendricks, actor*

"To this day my arms, shoulders, breasts, and thighs are fuller. I have a little mommy pouch, and I'm in no rush to get rid of it. I think it's real. . . . Right now, my little FUPA and I feel like we are meant to be."—*Beyoncé, singer/ producer*

"This body is resilient. It can endure all kinds of things. My body offers me the power of presence. My body is powerful." —Roxane Gay, author

"I'm fat and happy. Don't force your ideals on me and my body because I'm doing just fine without your approval." —Tess Holiday, model

"I am allowed to look sexy, feel sexy and be in love. I am worthy of all those things, and so are you." —Mary Lambert, singer

TRANS GIRLS, BOIS, AND NONBINARY PEOPLE ____

We see you. Maybe you're asking:

How am I supposed to love a body that betrays me? It is my body that makes people misgender me. That constantly communicates that I am someone I am not. How can I love a body that is not my own? When it is the cause of my dysphoria? I can't celebrate my bodily changes like other girls, because the changes my body is going through tells the world that they get to define me rather than me defining myself. I can't love a body like mine when I don't see people like me represented in the media. When I don't see people like me being loved. How am I supposed to love this body when it's the reason why I have to go with the boys in gym and not the other girls? When it is the reason that the members of the Girls Empowerment Club side-eyed me when I came to the last meeting. My body hides who I really am and makes other people predetermine who they think they see. How can I love a body that makes me invisible?

So here's the thing. The world has limiting notions about gender. This is not your fault. Figuring out how to love your trans or nonbinary body when you have all these feelings to navigate is not something anyone can do for you. You're going to have to do what you need to do to love your body on your own terms. And that doesn't mean you have to love your body as-is. It means you get to do that shit your own way! And let us tell you, baby, when you do . . . your body is a gift! When you construct a self-identity that makes sense to you, you make it possible for all of us to define ourselves for ourselves. Your acts of self-love take the medical community head-on and declare that nobody gets to define you but you. Not even your body gets to define you. You are who you say you are. We define our damn selves. When you love your body, you make us create more expansive versions of girlhood. Where would feminism be without you?!

Words to Live By

> "I get to decide how my body shows up in any space. When I'm walking into a place like the [Golden] Globes, I want to make it very clear that how I show up is to further the freedom of everybody." —Indya Moore, actor

> "I didn't want anyone to have control over how people saw me. I wanted to have that power myself." —Indya Moore

> "For me, the transgender thing is the reality of my life. It's the reality of my existence and it's something that I've come to believe is beautiful about me." —Laverne Cox, actor

> "My body, my clothes, and my makeup are on purpose, just as I am on purpose." —Janet Mock, writer/director

> "Self-definition and self-determination is about the many varied decisions that we make to compose and journey toward ourselves, about the audacity and strength to proclaim, create, and evolve into who we know ourselves to be. It's okay if your personal definition is in a constant state of flux as you navigate the world." —Janet Mock

DISABLED GIRL . . . ⎯⎯⎯⎯⎯⎯⎯⎯⎯⎯⎯⎯⎯⎯⎯⎯

We see you! Maybe you're asking:

How can I love this body when it is a constant reminder of what I can't do? How can I love a body that the world tells me is broken? When so many people pray for their children to not be born like me? How can I love a body that I rarely see on TV, in elected office, or in history? How can I love a body that I never see being loved? When people like me are only used to tell stories of inspiration and triumph, but not of everyday shit like shopping with your friends and arguing with your parents? How can I love my body when people see me and automatically read me as mentally incapable? When it is the reason why strangers stare at me but don't really see me? How can I love a body that makes me invisible?

We hear you! And we see you! This road to loving yourself is not going to be an easy journey for you. But one thing you should remember is that the challenges you face have less to do with your body and more to do with the fact that we (not us, but you know what we mean) designed a world that only certain bodies can move through. Remember what we said earlier about structures? You have to remember that they are the problem, not you!

And you need to know that your body is a whole-ass gift! When you love your body, you show us that there is no one way to be a body in this world. There is no such thing as normal! We are different people, in different bodies, doing different ish. You also show us that the only way we survive structures is in community. When you need help and ask for it unapologetically, you remind all of us to reject the individualism that white-supremacist capitalist patriarchy so desperately wants us to embrace. Who the hell wants to do this alone?!

Tips

OK. So you know how supermodel Winnie Harlow embraced her vitiligo and made space for other people with that skin condition to do the same? (I mean, there are so many young girls proudly showing off their vitiligo and we are here for all of it!) Well, there's that same energy in the disability community. There are people with all kinds of disabilities who are out there living their best lives and documenting it for the world to see. We don't know about y'all but we think there's something super powerful about seeing things that you wanted to hide about yourself reflected back at you through the confidence of others. The internet makes it so easy to find your tribe. Here are some people to follow to get you started curating a feed that speaks to you:

@itslololove: Lauren Spencer is a sista in a wheelchair who blogs about fashion and disability. Yassss!

@jessicaoutofthecloset: Jessica Kellgren-Fozard is a deaf, queer YouTuber and Instagrammer who shares funny videos and cool photos, adding what she says is "vintage fabulousness to a life with disabilities and chronic illnesses." We stan!

@aaron＿philip: Aaron Philip is a Black, trans, disabled model living with cerebral palsy. Cool fact: she got signed to Elite models before she even finished high school. #Goals

@jillianmercado: Jillian Mercado is an American fashion model, and as a wheelchair user, she is one of the few professional models who has a physical disability in the fashion industry. Homegirl is serving all the looks on her feed! Werk!

@viktoriamodesta: Viktoria Modesta defines herself as a bionic artist exploring modern identity through performance, fashion, avant-garde visuals, technology, and science. Her page is super dope.

CHRONICALLY ILL GIRL . . . ───────────────

We see you. Maybe you're asking:

How am I supposed to love this body that causes me so much pain? That can't do what I will it to do? That surprises me and keeps me from living my life? How am I supposed to love this body when it is a constant reminder of my fragility? That I am not like other young people? When a sickness has caused me to change so much physically that I don't feel pretty? How can I love a body when it is the reason why I have to let my friends and family down again because I'm too sick to do what I promised I would do? How can I love a body that ruins my vacation plans and makes me have to give up my tickets to the Billie Eilish concert I waited months for? How can I love my body when it can't even make it through the day without medication that sometimes makes me sicker than the illness? When I spend more time budgeting my energy than my allowance? And how can I love my body when it betrays me by looking healthy, causing me to have to defend how bad I feel to people who keep asking me to "suck it up"? How can I love a body that makes me invisible?

We hear you and we see you. We are not going to tell you that everything is going to be all right, because we don't know that and it may not be true. But we will tell you that when you practice self-love, your body is a gift! You have shown us the true meaning of carpe diem. Because you cannot predict how you'll feel from day to day, you have taught us to live each day to the fullest. You have also taught us that it is OK to slow down, and you've shown us how to do so. You have modeled the self-care that feminists have touted for years. When you love your body, you teach all of us that our bodies are constantly communicating to us and show us how to listen.

You may find community and solace in the term "spoonie." A spoonie is someone who suffers from a chronic illness. Spoon theory was developed by Christine Miserandino, an award-winning blogger and patient advocate, as a way to describe to her friend what it is like living with lupus. She laid out a handful of spoons on the table and explained that the spoons symbolize all of her daily energy. Everything she does each day, no matter how little thought goes into it, depletes from her energy supply. Getting out of bed, getting dressed, and eating all deplete energy. Sound relatable? Because you have fewer spoons than your healthy friends, going to class, step team practice, and doing your homework make you even more tired. By the end of the day you may be operating from a deficit, while they still have spoons remaining.

If spoon theory seems to fit you, take a look online at the community of people who are posting around that term. There are also hashtags dedicated to specific chronic illnesses, so try searching a hashtag and find your people.

WHAT WOULD CARDI, LIZZO, AND MEG DO?

Cardi B, Lizzo, and Megan Thee Stallion come together to teach all of us how to love our bodies better.

> BITCHES WOULD BE LIKE, "OH MY GOD, BUT WHY HER?". . . 'CAUSE I'M A MOTHERFUCKING VIBE. UNFORGETTABLE, UNEXPLAINABLE.
>
> —Cardi B

Cardi B teaches us how we need to act when we see a mirror. Sometimes you have to fake it until you make it. We want you to stand in front of the mirror every day and tell yourself you're beautiful. It's OK if you don't believe it. It will come. There may not be another person in the world who thinks you are beautiful, but when you think you're beautiful, nobody can tell you anything. Before you know it, you are going to be "walkin' past the mirror, Ooh damn, I'm fine."

> I WANT PEOPLE TO FEEL THAT CLOSENESS, BECAUSE IF YOU CAN LOVE ME AS MUCH AS YOU DO WITHOUT KNOWING ME, AND WITHOUT ME BEING LIKE THIS ARCHETYPE OF MODERN BEAUTY IN MEDIA, THEN YOU CAN LOVE YOURSELF.
>
> —Lizzo

Then we have Lizzo. Sometimes you can find beauty in others that you can't see in yourself. The wonder of social media is that you can curate your own feed. You don't have to be subjected to what other people say is beautiful. You're in control. Fill your page with other people like you who are already on the path of loving their bodies. Love them until you can find the strength to love yourself.

> SOMETIMES YOU JUST GOT TO REMIND PEOPLE THAT YOU'RE MAGICAL AND EVERYTHING ABOUT YOU DOWN TO YOUR VAGINA AND TO YOUR TOES IS MAGICAL.
>
> —Megan Thee Stallion

And last we have Ms. Hot Girl Summer herself, Megan Thee Stallion. Megan reminds us of the power of the twerk. Twerking crosses all gender lines and sexual orientations. Men twerk. Black college bands bust a move. And some of the people who really put twerking on the map were gender nonconforming people like Big Freedia and trans women like Katey Red. People of all abilities have experienced the exhilaration of a gyration. It is a reminder that our bodies are free.

There's nothing like the feeling of our bodies moving to a beat. Nothing feels as good as nailing a dance move after practicing it for weeks. Twerking puts our energy into what our bodies can do. Not what they look like.

So, when all else fails, remember Cardi B, Lizzo, and Meg, and you'll be all right.

BROWN SKIN GIRL

AS A BLACK WOMAN, AS A LIGHT-SKINNED
BLACK WOMAN, IT'S IMPORTANT THAT I'M
USING MY PRIVILEGE, MY PLATFORM TO
SHOW YOU HOW MUCH BEAUTY THERE IS IN
THE AFRICAN AMERICAN COMMUNITY. I AM
HOLLYWOOD'S, I GUESS YOU COULD SAY,
"ACCEPTABLE" VERSION OF A BLACK GIRL,
AND THAT HAS TO CHANGE.

–Zendaya

THE TRUE FOCUS OF REVOLUTIONARY CHANGE IS
NEVER MERELY THE OPPRESSIVE SITUATIONS
WHICH WE SEEK TO ESCAPE, BUT THAT PIECE
OF THE OPPRESSOR WHICH IS PLANTED DEEP
WITHIN EACH OF US.

–Audre Lorde

IN A LAND THAT LOVES ITS BLOND, BLUE-EYED CHILDREN, WHO WEEPS FOR THE DREAMS OF A BLACK GIRL?

—Toni Morrison

WHAT IS COLORISM ANYWAY?

It seems that every few months, social media erupts in an age-old debate in communities of color around colorism. It usually goes a little something like this: Celebrity X publicly declares that they prefer light-skinned Black women over dark-skinned Black women, Black women with darker skin get rightfully offended and take the celebrity to task, these women are then called sensitive and told they are overreacting, fans of Celebrity X and other celebrities rush to the defense of Celebrity X, someone inserts a question like "What's wrong with having preferences?" and then the conversation gradually fades away. Meanwhile, the dark-skinned women who were hurt by such sentiments are silenced and left to wonder, again, where's the love for women who look like them?

Communities of color have been talking about *colorism*—the jacked-up systems of ideas that favor lighter skin tones over darker ones and awards privileges to people based on their proximity to whiteness—for a very, very, very long time. Colorism is a form of internalized white supremacy. In a world where white people are considered the standard for beauty and goodness, lighter skin tones, because of their proximity to whiteness, have been deemed more valuable, beautiful, and worthy. One study found that lighter-skinned people even received lesser prison sentences than darker-skinned people! Light-skinned privilege is real.

And while Black people didn't create the practice of colorism, we've most definitely done our part in holding it up by internalizing this form of racism. You might find a friend or relative remarking during the summer months about how they "need to stay out of the sun so they don't get too dark." That is internalized white supremacy showing up as colorism.

Black people, like other people of color, already struggle for representation. When we finally do get there, the people who get a seat at the table are not reflective of the diversity of our communities.

You can really see this play out in the media, where there is a disproportionate number of light-skinned Black women who are chosen to represent the ideal image of Black beauty. It's like the closer you are to Eurocentric definitions of beauty, the more props you get. Meanwhile, our sisters with dark skin, broad noses, and kinky hair struggle to get any play. Some companies have even gone as far as lightening Black women in their ads to make them appear even closer to this beauty norm. When dark girls are cast, they tend to be relegated to the roles that make them appear to be hypersexual or angry, or they are relegated to service roles like maids and nannies. Although there's nothing inherently wrong with these roles, we want representation that is as diverse as our real lives. Even when positive characters are created to be dark-skinned, the actors cast to play them are light-skinned women. Like, isn't Storm from X-Men supposed to be of Kenyan descent? Why is she always played by a light-skinned actress. Sheesh, can a dark girl live?!

And look, no one is saying light skin isn't beautiful. But everybody already knows that! That's the issue! Imagine, though, what it must feel like to never see an image of beauty for your race that reflects you. Imagine what it must be like to interact with media—a major site where our social validation occurs—and see those of your hue degraded, demeaned, or just straight-up absent, as opposed to celebrated and held up as #Goals. That can have a major impact on one's sense of self.

And this isn't just a problem for Black people. Unfortunately, colorism is a global phenomenon. Brittney was shocked when a Malaysian roommate told her during a summer trip to South Korea that South Koreans were considered fair-skinned Asians, while Malaysians were seen as darker and less beautiful. All around the world we encounter the belief that value and beauty are determined by proximity to whiteness. Skin-bleaching products are a multimillion-dollar industry around the world. While Afro-Latinx representation is on the rise, the most consistent examples of Latinas making it to the mainstream tend to be those with light skin. Dark-skinned Indian actors struggle to find lead roles in Bollywood. White supremacy is a global problem and anti-Blackness is everywhere!

So while some feminists think that railing against the patriarchy means declaring that beauty should not matter at all, we think that a better solution is recognizing that beauty comes in many different forms. Whether you are light-skinned, dark-skinned, cinnamon-toned, cocoa-butter brown, mahogany, onyx, shea-butter brown or anything in between, your Black is beautiful.

WHY COLORISM MATTERS

For the Brown girls, having to navigate this, along with the hundreds of other things you are trying to figure out in girlhood, is tough! And the grass may seem greener on the other side. But the truth is, none of us have it easy, and there's really no sense in us trying to one-up the other over who has it better or worse.

Our dark-skinned sisters have been denied access to ideals of beauty that reflect their hue, have been marginalized when they are present, and have been denied the economic benefits of being close to whiteness. Our light-skinned sisters have had to deal with misplaced resentment that has sometimes resulted in violence and feelings of alienation stemming from constantly having their race questioned. To move forward, we're going to have to deal with all of it—the hurt, the privilege, the resentment, and the desire to be accepted.

A part of crushing girlhood is building our own definitions of what is beautiful and celebrating what makes us unique. But how in the hell are we supposed to do that when people keep imposing standards of beauty on us that we don't fit?! While these are not narratives that come from our communities, we are the ones that are forced to navigate them, and that shit is in the way. We're out here playing roles in a script that we didn't even write! We can no longer allow a preexisting script to define us.

HOW TO CRUSH GIRLHOOD WITHOUT BEING COLORIST

Here's what we have to do to get on with the business of defining beauty for ourselves:

KEEP YOUR HEAD ON A SWIVEL The first thing we have to do is pay attention to how colorism is affecting the world around us. Notice who gets to represent your culture and then ask why. Who gets to play the majority of leading roles for your race? Who gets to be the love interest in movies and in music videos? Who's on the arm of your favorite celebrity? But don't just question media. Ask yourself: What have the great thinkers and leaders of your race looked like? What was the hue of the notable "firsts" of your race?

GET YOUR LIFE The truth is, we all have the potential to perpetuate colorism, so it's important that we commit to self-exploration. We may say things like "that's a waste of light skin," or declare our disdain for celebrities of a particular hue. We have to go deep within and notice when we are doing these things, and then work really hard to reject our own anti-Blackness. We have to erase the residue of centuries of messages telling us a certain skin complexion, hair texture, or nose width is ideal and force ourselves to expand our notions of beauty. It's a practice.

TELL 'EM, "BOY, BYE" We're done listening to people who seek to separate us and force us into their rigid definitions of beauty. If the people we support don't want to reckon with their messed-up standards of beauty, then we no longer have to support them. Next time a celebrity exhibits anti-Black sentiments, shut that shit down! There are plenty of music artists, actors, and designers to choose from. We don't have to ride for people who aren't riding for us. On the flipside ...

WE GOOD OVER HERE We have to remember to focus on the positive. Sometimes we can get so focused on which celebrities aren't rocking with us that we lose sight of those who are. Whenever ugly things are said, there is always someone, somewhere, who is trying to be a light. There is someone who is validating the feelings of those who are hurt and there is someone bold enough to be an example of a different model of Black beauty by embracing aspects of themselves that are typically shunned. Tika Sumpter, Lupita Nyong'o, Aja Naomi King, and the 2019 Miss Universe, Zozibini Tunzi, are just a few examples of folks repping hard for the dark girls and speaking openly about loving their ebony skin. Beyoncé's "Brown Skin Girl" is an ode to and an anthem for all the dark-skinned girls and a reminder that at the end of the day, women of color will hold one another down. And as much as things have stayed the same, there is also a lot changing. The creators of *Black Panther* deserve major props for having a cast of almost all dark-skinned Black women. And we are so excited to see young queens like Skai Jackson, Marsai Martin, and Shahadi Wright Joseph diversify the image of young #BlackGirlMagic.

RUBBER AND GLUE Whatever you do, don't internalize the messages! Remember that saying "I'm rubber, you're glue. Whatever you say bounces off of me and sticks onto you"? Say that, or whatever you need to say to not let these messages get into your head. In today's age of social media, we can curate our own feeds and find people who represent a beauty that makes sense to us. You can hop on Instagram and search the hashtag #Melanin and see Black people in all of our glorious beauty. Dark girls don't have to only consume the mainstream media that is presented to them on television screens, magazine covers, and the background of music videos.

A NOTE TO THE DARK-SKINNED GIRLS

Know that you are abundantly beautiful. Your skin is smooth like silk. Your ebony is deep and glorious. And have you seen yourself in yellow?! Baby, you shut it all the way down! People need to really stop acting like pretty dark-skinned girls are an anomaly. Next time somebody tries to tell you, "You're pretty for a dark-skinned girl," you tell them, "I'm pretty period, bih!"

A NOTE TO THE LIGHT-SKINNED GIRLS

The global aspect of this also means that it plays out differently in different communities, especially for those of you who may be mixed-race. You can have light-skin privilege in the Black community but feel the full brunt of your Blackness in the other community you call your own. Having to move between two worlds does something to your psyche. We get it. And we want to say, you do not have to prove your Blackness or Brownness to anybody. Blackness has always been every color of the spectrum, and it is as much a political identity as it is a physical one. We absolutely need you to acknowledge that you have light-skinned privilege. However, don't feed into people's desires to police your Blackness. It is what it is. Keep embracing the mahogany in your own skin while also giving a resounding "yasss queen" to your dark-skinned sisters when they do the same. Also, be leery of people who state their preference for girls that look like you while also looking down on dark-skinned women at the same damn time. You can give compliments or be attracted to someone without disrespecting an entire portion of our community. We're not interested in contests that put us on top of a Black-girl hierarchy. Thank you, next.

BIG EACH OTHER UP The main thing we have to do is stick together as homegirls. Even though colorism affects all POC, it affects men and women very differently. Sometimes, Black men and boys become complicit in perpetuating these troubling narratives because they assume that they get to determine what's beautiful. You know how we disrupt that? We put forth a sisterhood that is even more powerful! We all suffer emotional pain when we get picked over like sneakers. We also all struggle with seeing ourselves as beautiful when the ideal image of beauty for centuries has been white. We don't have to reinforce society's standards of beauty. We can create our own more expansive definitions and own it. Learning to love ourselves is a lifelong endeavor. We can do it together!

HOL' UP

A word on preferences: It never fails that when these conversations pop off, someone brings up preferences, so let us say a quick word about that. Our preferences don't just come out of the blue. They are often shaped by a host of factors that include our families, our peers, and the media we consume. Thus, our preferences are not exempt from critique. Preference for a particular skin tone, body type, hair type, or facial feature is informed by the many messages we receive regarding good/bad, ugly/pretty, acceptable/deplorable. We can't cap like public figures don't have a lot of influence over our decisions. They influence the clothes we wear, accessories we rock, and even how we do our makeup. So when a celebrity uses their platform to declare the kind of woman they are attracted to or find undesirable, they are using their power to do something more than simply state their preferences. They are shaping our ideals of beauty.

LET ME GRAB MY HOOPS

(AND OTHER TALISMANS)

A talisman is a small object that you use to give you power, to connect with your god, guides, ancestors, spirits. It can also be used as a confidence booster. Even though Black girls don't always say it, we often implicitly use things to give us a little extra pep in our step on tough days, a little extra boost to help us channel our power and project it to the world.

I (Brittney) never leave the house without my hoop earrings. In my baby pics, I'm rocking tiny hoops! And as I've gotten older, the hoops have gotten larger, but I stay rockin' 'em. They never go out of style, they can be jazzy or plain, and they are the thing that tells my body that I'm ready to go out and face the world. You can rock hoops with a name plate and different shapes, ovals, doorknockers, you name it.

I (Chanel) feel my most confident when I put on my mother's flower ring and/ or a pair of Air Max or Jordans. The ring connects me to my mother's spirit and reminds me my ancestors are with me. The kicks make me feel connected to my 'hoods and remind me of the ways we created our own fashion, culture, and style.

I (Susana) never leave home without my lipstick. Lipstick is my thing. Growing up, I didn't always feel entitled to feeling pretty, but these days I reject that nonsense. When I paint my lips in shades of brown, purple, red, or whatever I feel like rocking, I feel like the badass powerhouse femme that I am.

We are all riffing on the same idea. So, what's your talisman, the thing that makes you ready to go out in the world, kick butt, and take names? Is it a ring, a chain, earrings, a particular lip color, a bad shoe, a Jesus piece, a crystal, a signature pen, your notebook, or a small memento of a dope memory or experience?

What's that thing that reminds you of who you are, why you're here, and how powerful you are?

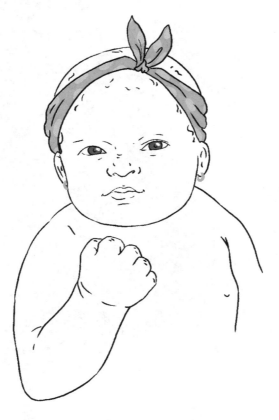

3

WHAT ABOUT YOUR FRIENDS

(AND FAMILY AND 'EM)?

THE FAM

*A*s you continue to live life as a feminist, there will be people who will try to tell you that feminists are anti-family and that being a feminist is incompatible with supporting family. They will try to convince you that because we do not believe we should completely sacrifice our lives to our family, or that our only important identities are as mothers, daughters, sisters, and wives, that we do not care about the family—and even worse, that we want to destroy it. They are going to try to tell you that the family is the realm of conservatives and the party of "family values." But this could not be further from the truth.

WHO THE HECK IS "THEY"?

You may be asking—but you know exactly who they are. DJ Khaled tells us "they don't want you to be great" as a way to talk about the haters and the way that some people try to keep you from your path to success. When it comes to feminism, "they" are the people who want you to believe that feminism is an evil ideology that seeks to destroy all that is good in society. They don't want you to be a feminist, so they try to target the things you love and tell you that feminists want to ruin it. They are wrong. Feminism is rooted in loving and making a better place for all people. Don't listen to "they." They are stupid.

The personal is political, right? Well, there's nothing more personal than the family. As feminists, we do not think that family is a relationship that is separate from the state (meaning the government, whether local or national). The state is all up in the family—trying to determine who gets married, which family setups can get tax breaks, who can be on your healthcare benefits (your spouse of two weeks can but your mother cannot), who has parental rights, and who gets to make decisions about whether to bring children into the world. The state cares an awful lot about families, and therefore so do we as feminists.

We care that the Black family unit was devastated by the separation of enslaved parents from their children and the inability of enslaved people to have their marriages legally recognized.

We care that this still happens in the ways that welfare policies often take away benefits from women who are partnered.

We care about the number of Black children who are in foster care while their mothers are incarcerated if they can't pay fines or legal fees. (We wonder what would happen if those state payouts for foster parents went to help parents support their own families instead.)

So, yeah, we treat the family as the social institution that it is. As feminists, it is our job to examine the social institutions that govern the lives of women and girls.

When it comes to the family, raising children and caring for domestic responsibilities are seen as cis women's biological destiny, simply because we may have wombs. Look, there's nothing wrong with nurturing. Chanel, like many feminists, loves being a mother and enjoys the nurturing aspect that comes with caring for her children. (Feminist mothering communities are totally a thing. There are a ton of blogs and influencers out there who are thinking about this.) However, she doesn't think that this should be her destiny or the destiny of other women simply because of their identity as women. Her brother is also quite the nurturer and will be the first one making soup and grabbing the Vicks when her nephew is sick.

Feminists care so much about the family that you can often find us at the forefront of fighting for policies and cultural changes that benefit families. (And when we're on the front lines advocating for families, where "they" at, tho?) For example, does your mom work outside the home and is she able to keep the money she makes? You can thank a feminist for that. Was she able to return to work after taking time off when she had your baby brother? You can thank a feminist for that. Was your dad able to get parental leave as well? Yep. Feminists did that. Was your grandmother able to divorce your grandfather when she felt that the relationship was no longer loving and beneficial to her? You can thank a feminist for that. Is your big sister able to breastfeed your niece in public? You're welcome. Feminists did that too.

What about your pops? Did your parents decide that it made more sense for your mom to keep her higher paying job while your dad stayed home with you and your siblings? Feminists are the ones who fought tooth and nail for us to be done with BS gendered divisions in household labor. We thought that women should share some of the burden of breadwinning and men should share some of the burden of housework. Feminists fought for egalitarian households, and the queer community gave us models for what it looks like to create a division of household labor that isn't rooted in gender. Is your stepdad a nurse or a teacher? Who do you think was on the front lines pushing for these occupations to not be seen as "women's work" and then further devalued?

There is still much work to do, but you better believe that it is feminists who are fighting every single day for universal childcare, paid parental leave for all parents, universal healthcare, and free colleges—policies that families want to see. We broke up the idea that women naturally want to raise children and men naturally do not. We reject the lie that queer and trans folk are anti-family. Who do you think is riding about the maternal mortality rate for women who are trying to bring babies into the world? Feminists are not only pushing for policies that make sure these women get to go home to their families and that giving birth is not a death sentence, we are also are becoming doulas and making sure we do what we can to support these women.

"They" got us twisted. We don't hate the family or the men in our families. We hate the underlying patriarchal structures that reproduce and reinforce the male, capitalist privilege that runs throughout our families. We don't think our mother should have to submit to our father for no other reason than because he is a man. If she is a financial adviser and he is an elementary school teacher, shouldn't she be the one to handle the money and he the one to take the lead on teaching Junior to read? We don't think girls should be expected to tend to the domestic tasks like laundry and dishwashing and boys should be doing the more "manly" work, like mowing the lawn and washing the car, simply because of their gender. And we definitely don't think the toys that teach children how to nurture others (dolls), care for themselves (kitchen sets), and take care of their homes (cleaning toys), should be marketed only to girls. What kind of message does that send?

See? Feminists care a great deal about the family. We just do not think that the family should be immune from the feminist principles we fight for everywhere else. We want families that are centered on principles of justice and freedom and are free from white-supremacist, capitalist, patriarchal norms. We want families that are truly built around principles of love, nurture, support, and collectivity. This is our fight. Nothing more and nothing less.

At the end of the day, feminism is about relationships, and when we were your age, most of our relationships centered on our families. Families can be a source of love, support, stability, and joy. They can also be a source of pain, confusion, unhappiness, and, unfortunately, even abuse. Many families contain a bit of many of these elements (and more), so it is no secret that many of us have complicated relationships with our families.

We gathered a sampling of some of the biggest issues girls face within their family and provide some feminist advice that we hope will help you navigate this institution.

OMG. I seriously can't with my parents always pressing me about chores. It seems like my parents just don't understand that I have band, chess club, a part-time job, and maintain a very high GPA. Do they not want me to get into college? How can I get my parents to chill and let me off the hook when it comes to doing stuff around the house?

This is a tricky one because we feminists have been quite vocal that women's work should not be relegated to the realm of the home. We belong in politics, business, education, healthcare, media, and wherever else we want to be. But that being said, we think you should do your chores.

Here's why. One, we believe in collectivizing everything and that the home is a key site of that . We work together to take care of our homes and to take care of the people in the home. Everyone who is able to contribute time, money, and energy in the maintenance of the home should be doing so. That labor should not fall on one person.

Two, we actually really value the unpaid work that goes on in the house. Every year, Salary.com calculates how much money a stay-at-home parent should make. In 2019, that calculation was over $178,000 per year. Stay-at-home parents act as chauffeurs, chefs, nannies, tutors, housecleaners, beauticians, and so on. But that kind of labor—like most work that is deemed "women's work"—goes unrecognized and unvalued in a capitalist society. But that's not how we roll. Your schoolwork and extracurricular activities are very important, but they are not more important than washing the dishes.

Now, if you are doing chores around the house and the boys in your household are not, that's a problem. Or if there is a gendered division of labor that means your brother never has to do to the laundry and you are not allowed to wash the cars, yeah, we might want to question that. You can try to encourage your family to divide the household labor based on strengths and interests, and maybe tell your parents that you think you and your siblings should learn how to do everything so that you can all be self-reliant.

When I look on TV, it seems that the ideal family has a mom and a dad and kids. My family looks nothing like that. I live with my mom, my aunt, my little cousin, and my grandmother. I love my family more than anything, but I can't help but feel a little bit embarrassed that my family isn't normal. What can I do?

Before shows like *Raven's Home* portrayed two single mothers living together to raise their children or *Andi Mack* showed a young girl being raised by her grandma, the ideal American family in popular culture consisted of a mother, father, 2.5 kids, and a dog. They lived in the suburbs and drove a station wagon. The mom stayed at home and cooked and cleaned while the dad went out and worked. The kids, a brother and a sister, were perfectly clean-cut and never got into trouble or even got dirty. It probably goes without saying that this family was white and middle-class.

This was the fantasy of the nuclear family, and it was just that—a fantasy. Real families come in a variety of different shapes, sizes, and configurations. It could be just you and your mom or your dad. Maybe you have a gang of siblings, one parent, and your auntie lives with you too. Your granny might be raising you. Maybe you're adopted. Or maybe you've come through the foster-care system. You might be part of a blended family with stepparents and stepsiblings. You may have two moms or two dads. Maybe one of your parents is incarcerated and you don't really get to see them often.

Chanel grew up in a brownstone in Brooklyn with her mother and brother, as well as her grandmother, aunt, two cousins, and a houseful of more cousins and her great-aunt right next door. While she was in grad school, she and her brother raised her nephew together for many years. For Brittney, it was just her and her mom for a while until her stepfather came along. Susana grew up with her mom and sisters and went back and forth between the United States and Jamaica. There are all kinds of family arrangements that exist for a variety of reasons. Some people make their family solely out of love. Others may make choices based on economic realities. Still more may structure the family around caring for elderly family members or babies. There's no right way to do it, and just because your fam doesn't fit the mythical ideal, that doesn't mean it's not really family.

And different family configurations have different challenges. You might come from a big family with lots of siblings, cousins, aunts, and uncles. And while it's cool to have so many people around, you might also wish for a quiet corner to yourself and maybe even envy your friends who have smaller families. Maybe your family is small, just you and one parent. You might feel lucky to have an intense bond with one other person, but you may also feel isolated and envy your friends who have a big family with tons of siblings and cousins to hang with.

The thing to remember here is that patriarchy tells us a lie when it says that the nuclear family is the "normal" family structure and the one that we should all be aspiring to. The nuclear family is the structure that is supported by laws and tax breaks and other benefits, like being able to share insurance plans. But just because the nuclear family is the one that is supported by the state, that doesn't make it right or even "normal." Other family configurations are just as important, and we would bet most people probably live in families that are not nuclear. As feminists, our task is to uphold the right to make your family look the way you want it to look and to fight for the legitimacy of those family arrangements.

Be proud that the people in your family chose to stare down the barrel of patriarchy and build their own structure for parenting together.

Me and my cousin are the same age and we've always been inseparable. However, ever since we went to high school, we don't really hang or talk as much and we don't really share the same interests. Should I try to work on our relationship or just let it be?

Growing up usually means navigating transitions with your family. You might have been super cool with your cousins when you were kids, but now that you're older you might find you have less in common with them. We think that sometimes we put too much emphasis on the family and perhaps we need to evaluate our cousin, sibling, and even parent relationships the same way we do our friendships. There are times when people simply grow apart or when a relationship is no longer a good one for you. The idea that these people hold a special place—even if they are mean, or violent, or just not who you want to rock with—is kind of weird. "Never go against the family!" *Soooo* . . . the family can just do whatever, and I'm supposed to just take it? Nah. I'm good. Once you figure out what the requirements are for people having access to you, you get to put them around your cousins and them too.

But on the flip side, if this is a relationship that matters to you, then you can't just think it's going to always just be there just 'cause y'all are family. It doesn't work like that. All relationships take work. We shouldn't sacrifice ourselves for the sake of the family, but we also shouldn't take our familial relationships for granted. While you're thinking about this with your cousin now, you may have to evaluate your relationship with your parents, grandparents, and siblings in the future as you figure out what's best for your own well-being.

CHOSEN FAMILY

You've probably heard folks say stuff like "blood is thicker than water," right? People say that to mean that your biological family is more important or should be more important than anyone else. And while that may be the case for some people, it's definitely not true for everyone. Another popular saying is that "you can't choose your family." But, lowkey, you can. Your "family of origin" is the family you were born or adopted into, but you can also have a "chosen family." Members of your chosen family are just that—folks you choose. They could be related or unrelated to you. They could be folks you're in the marching band with or on the softball team with. Maybe y'all play video games together or follow each other on Instagram. You have stuff in common, support each other, and hold each other down. Chosen family is important to everyone but can be especially vital if you are queer, trans, or nonbinary. When you don't fit into society's mold of how to be, it's important to have an affirming community that you can be a part of.

My family does not feel like a safe space for me and could even be described as abusive. I'm a long way from being able to move out on my own, so what can I do to protect myself in the meantime?

Family life is particularly difficult if your family is not a safe space. Maybe you are queer, trans, or nonbinary and your folks are hostile to your sexuality or gender identity. Maybe your family is very religious but it is a faith you no longer want to follow. It might be difficult to find a family member to confide in if they think something is not OK with you simply existing as you are or who you want to be. Maybe somebody in your family is abusing you, either emotionally, physically, or sexually, and you feel safer away from them. Maybe your primary caregiver has untreated mental illness or is suffering from addiction and these things manifest in ways that are unsafe for you. These sorts of issues go beyond "normal" family disputes.

If you're experiencing abuse or neglect within your family, there are a few things you should know: First, none of this is your fault; you did absolutely nothing to deserve it. You are valuable and deserving of love, support, and safety. Second, it is not your job to fix a family member who is suffering from illness or addiction, or who is hostile or abusive. You also have to resist the urge to assume that their inability to stop or go get help indicates that they don't love you enough. They have deep-rooted struggles they are going to have to work through, and making it your responsibility is too much for you to bear. All you can do is be compassionate, but also strengthen yourself so you can survive.

If there is someone else in your family or in your community that you can trust, reach out to them to see if you can find a safer space as soon as possible. For many of you, the thought of social workers coming into your home is terrifying, and the truth is, there is some history of them causing more harm than good for children of color. Maybe you've been in a group home before and have decided that what you're experiencing now pales in comparison to what you experienced there. These aren't easy choices, and you're going to have to work with a trusted adult to figure out when your situation has reached a point of needing more serious intervention.

The other thing you want to do is try your best to get busy, and fast. That means join a ton of extracurricular activities and get an afterschool job so you have legitimate reasons to be home as infrequently as possible. When you can, go over to your friend's house or chill at another trusted family member's house as much as possible. The goal here is to reduce contact where you can. Your new motto: *I'm just here to eat, bathe, and sleep.* And as soon as you get old enough to go, you're going to have to go. And then you can begin the very difficult work of figuring out how to love your family from afar and finding the ways that you can be a good daughter without opening yourself up to so much pain.

RESOURCES

Alateen is the Alcoholics Anonymous community for children of alcoholics (al-anon.org/newcomers/teen-corner-alateen/)

The Trevor Project for LGBTQ Youth is an organization that provides crisis intervention and suicide prevention for LGBTQ youth (thetrevor project.org)

National Alliance on Mental Illness (NAMI) offers free support programs and education for family members (nami.org)

Black Emotional and Mental Health Collective (BEAM) is an organization dedicated to the emotional and mental health of the Black community (beam.community)

Men Stopping Violence has resources for men who want to unlearn aspects of toxic masculinity (menstoppingviolence.org)

#MeToo movement founder Tarana Burke has a website with resources for survivors of sexual violence (justbeinc.wixsite.com/justbeinc/home)

RAINN (Rape, Abuse & Incest National Network) is the nation's largest anti-sexual-violence organization (rainn.org)

My father has raised me by himself most of my life, and it's always just been me and him. He's dated people in the past but it's never been really serious. But now he's dating someone new and he just told me that we're all moving in together. I told him I wasn't feeling it at all, and he seemed hurt but said that this is what we're doing. What should I do?

We completely understand where you are coming from, and we've been there or supported others through this transition. It's totally normal to be uncomfortable with such a dramatic shift. The family makeup you have now is stable, and who doesn't like stability? You and your pops have a good routine going, and maybe y'all have some disagreements here and there, but you'd rather fuss with him than some lady you don't even like very much.

But here's the thing: your parents deserve to be full humans who have all of their needs met. Remember, one of the lies that the patriarchy tells us is that we should be singularly devoted to our families, and especially our children.

When we were young, we could only see our parent's relationship with us. As we got older, we came to realize the ways that they need their own friendships, jobs, volunteer work, alone time, and so much more to fulfill them. This doesn't mean they love you less or that they aren't considering your needs and desires. It just means that your parents have needs that you cannot meet.

This is true for you too. You're also getting older and may have a boo thing of your own. You're definitely starting to spend less time at home with your dad. Should he just sit there and twiddle his thumbs while you hang at the mall? We have to work to see our parents as people and not just our moms and dads.

But one of the things you may be doing here is bracing yourself, because what if you come to love this—the two incomes means you get a bigger room, can take family vacays, and get more gear—and it falls apart? What if having someone else to talk about crushes and friendship feels nice, and then it goes away? One of the hardest truths in life is that all the good things that we want are things that require risks. As we take more risks, we become wiser about what is a healthy risk and what is not.

We also want you to remember what a therapist once told us: that "our fears and anxiety are not intuition and are not always true." You may have real trauma (maybe your dad's last girlfriend was pretty awful). But we don't want your trauma to shape the way you perceive every interaction. We always have a chance to write a new ending to the story.

My mom works a lot and relies on me to help care for my two younger siblings. I get them ready for school in the morning, walk them to the bus stop, help with homework after school, and get dinner started on my own. I feel like I'm actually the one raising them and I can't have a life of my own. How can I let my mom know that she had these kids, not me?

That's hella frustrating. You're trying to hang out with your homies, but your little sibs are ruining your whole vibe. You are not alone in this. Older children, especially older girl children, have historically been asked to take on some of the childcare responsibilities to help their families out. You're not wrong for feeling like this is unfair.

But make sure that when you're upset, you keep your anger directed at the system that makes it necessary for you to care for your younger siblings. Childcare is ridiculously expensive. In fact, the average national cost is around a whopping $860/month. That's a lot of money. So, some of your situation is because you are in a working-class family and your parents have limited economic resources. Unfortunately, many of our ideas of what functional families look like come from watching white middle-class families that quite frankly have more resources. So, the level of responsibility required of you is different.

So yeah. You should be frustrated. But that's more of a reason to fight for a world where there are good, safe, reliable, and free twenty-four-hour childcare options that parents feel good about using.

In the meantime, we think you can be honest with your family about the ways that this is affecting you, and maybe they can find some ways to give you some time off. You should also know that your friends probably don't mind as much as you think they do, and while they may not adjust all their plans because of your babysitting responsibilities, they're probably willing to roll with you to check out a movie with the kiddos. You should also really relish the moments that you can get some free time to chill with your friends or be by yourself. Hang in there, sis.

I have been dating my girlfriend for about six months now and I know I love her. However, one day my mom overheard me saying I love her and she said, "You're too young for love. You don't know nothing about love." I hate when my parents invalidate my feelings.

OMG! We really hated when our parents did this to us. Whenever we had feelings that were different from what they deemed appropriate, they would either ignore us or tell us what we were feeling was not real. You're not hot. You're not hungry. You just ate. Stop crying before I give you something to cry about (as if what we were crying about wasn't valid). That's just puppy love. You ain't hurt. Ugh.

We feel your pain. We always wanted to say, "How you gon' tell us how we feel? Are you in my body?" Like the meme says: Your feelings are valid simply because you feel them.

This isn't just something you should shrug off tho. If you're not diligent, this can lead to you questioning your own thoughts and feelings. It can also lead you to constantly seeking external validation from others, and in some cases can cause severe perfectionism. And what makes this more difficult to navigate is that most people have no idea that what they are doing is causing harm. We don't really do kids right. We constantly think that kids are incapable of independent thoughts and of deep feelings like love.

There is also a history of women being told that we just don't know stuff. It's one of the most consistent ways that patriarchy works. We go to the doctor and are told that physiological problems are just in our head or that we are over-exaggerating our pain. We get in relationships and are told that we need to "calm down" and that we are "reading too much into things." We are told that we don't remember a sexual assault that is "indelible in the hippocampus" of our brains (shout-out to Dr. Christine Blasey Ford). And don't get us started on mansplaining, where men who took only one physics class in college try to explain astrophysics to someone like renowned astrophysicist Jocelyn Bell Burnell. The audacity. It's all so exhausting.

Welcome to girlhood. What you're going to need to do is find a way to validate yourself and check your own emotions, thoughts, and experiences when it comes to figuring out how you feel about someone. Only you know how you feel and if those feelings of joy and admiration are indeed love. These are probably some of the most exciting emotions you've ever felt. We think that young people know their lives, and we trust girls to know what they are feeling. Plus, if you can love your mom and dad, why can't you love your boyfriend? If you are capable of loving your BFF, then why is it so hard to believe that you are capable of loving your girlfriend? Those early romances, whether they last or not, will inform how you think about relationships, and you may even learn new things about yourself. Young love is indeed real love, and it is valid.

My parents are entirely too strict. They have me on a super-tight curfew, won't let me talk to boys, and I can only see my friends at school functions. On top of that, they have super-high expectations for me to be perfect—I have to have perfect grades, join the right clubs, and get the right kind of internship. How can I get a little bit of freedom? Sheesh!

We'll probably lose some cool points on this one, but we're going to ask you to have a little empathy for your parents here. We're not saying that this doesn't suck, but we think you should try to see things from their perspective a little bit. It is scary as hell to raise Black and Brown children in this world. It's not that your parents don't want you to be free; they are afraid of the repercussions of that freedom. For that reason, they want to keep you close and want to do whatever they can to keep you safe.

For some of you, your parents are raising you in a completely different environment from what they are used to. Maybe they are new to this country. Before, you might have found it easier to comply with your immigrant parents' desires, but now you're getting older, you might chafe under the weight of all their expectations.

Or maybe your parents had a come-up and y'all were able to move out of the 'hood. They may be trying to figure out these new cultural norms themselves and want to keep you close because they don't know what to expect. We all know that there is no guarantee that any of this is going to work. Your parents know that violence lurks around every corner and there is no real way to protect our children—but dictating your curfew, who you hang with, and where you go gives them some semblance of control in a world where what happens to our young people is pretty random.

You also have to remember that families of color don't have the same generational wealth as our white counterparts, so when your parents are extra hard on you to get the right grades, join the right clubs and organizations, and be in the right social circles, they are trying to give you as many advantages as possible. Don't read this as simply respectability politics. They are trying to come up with individual solutions to systemic issues. We are not saying it's right or wrong. Hell, it's going to take a lot to get us free. We just want to give you some context about where they are coming from.

We also want to caution you against hating your parents and being overly hard on them. For us, you can't say that you're about the revolution if you're committed to seeing your parents as the enemy. It's fundamentally unfeminist and is straight out of the white-supremacist, patriarchal playbook. We question why some people's impetus is to say "eff my mother." We don't roll like that. We can be deeply critical of our parents and even put up boundaries around our relationships with our parents, but we make it a practice to try to see them with loving eyes. (This does not apply if your parent is abusive. We are in no way asking you to sympathize with abusers. We are inviting you to have the kind of grace that we all desire in situations where we may not be perfect. Most parents are doing the best that they can. Giving them a little bit of a break is OK.) Plus, a lot of times we are harder on the people who show up and try than we are on the people who don't. Our father may not even be around, but our mother gets all the smoke because she won't let us have a boyfriend? Make it make sense.

We do have a few tips for you. This is a good time for you to figure out how to advocate for yourself and practice some negotiation skills. What would it take for them to let you do some things? Maybe they'd be comfortable with a situational curfew that was contingent on the activity. So maybe after the school play you have to be home within thirty minutes of ending, but maybe you can stay out until one a.m. after prom. Maybe you can agree on some friends whom they trust or set up a meeting where they can meet your friends' parents. The goal here is to assure them that they have done a good job instilling good morals and values in you and that they can trust you.

And if that doesn't work, just remember trouble don't last always. One day you'll be grown.

My big sister really gets on my nerves. She's constantly picking on me and laughing at my fashion choices, and we often physically fight. Our family kind of shrugs it off and says stuff like it's just making me tougher. What can I do?

We allow a lot of inappropriate behavior to happen in sibling relationships (or relationships between cousins of similar ages). Not just nasty arguments but actual physical fighting.

Chanel grew up in a family where she, her brother, and her cousins fought viciously. Fighting was the way they handled all major conflicts, and they would fight over any and everything. "Take off my shoes," "Stop singing while I watch TV," and "Stop telling Nana all the time" were all occasions that led to blows. The fact that they handled conflict through violence normalized physical violence as the way to handle conflict with peers. (In fact, it was also totally normal for there to be fights in the schoolyard after school or during lunchtime.) We think as feminists we need to examine these familial relationships as sites of domestic violence and as places where we learn some troubling stuff about how we should be in relationships with one another.

But if it can be learned, then it can be unlearned. So, let us say this: You do not have to give people access to you when they're being mean to you. You really can limit contact with people who don't treat you right. You can also disengage and refuse to participate in violent behavior. You should also tell your family how this makes you feel, and even consider having a sit-down with your sister and letting her know that you want to find a new way for y'all to resolve conflicts. She might feel the same way that you do, but not know of another way. This way of engaging may be so ingrained in your family and your community that you may have to seek the help of a family therapist to give you some other tools that you all can adopt to manage conflicts.

Every Sunday after church, we go over to my grandmother's house. It was cool when I was little, but lately I really hate going because she always has something to say about my body. "Look at your breasts getting big," "I see your hips spreading, mmm-hmm," "You put on a little weight, didn't you?" Once she starts, then my aunties also think it's fair game. How can I get them to leave me alone?

Oh, the-family-all up-in-your-body bit. We've been there. You be wanting to say "Mind the business that pays you," but you don't want to get in trouble.

The one thing we'll say here is that as young feminists, you have to remember that you are often modeling a new way of being for a generation that didn't get to be as free as you. How you get to move in the world is foreign to them, and a bit scary. When Chanel first went natural, her grandmother would always find a way to comment on her hair, saying stuff like "When are you going to put a perm in it?" One day she was preparing for an interview for an internship that she and her grandmother were both hoping she would get. Her grandmother told her to make sure she didn't wear her hair in an afro. It was then that she realized that her grandmother's criticism was actually rooted in a fear that people wouldn't accept her. She wasn't just hating on Chanel; that kind of freedom wasn't available for her grandmother. Sometimes families are concerned about whether something will be respectable in the eyes of people in power. Chanel's grandmother had never seen a Black woman get very far wearing her natural hair. (Chanel wore her natural hair and got the job. It was fine.)

We have to see our families' critiques as a kind of love that makes them want to control things. Will we be accepted if we get "too fat"? Will people like us if we rock our kinky hair? This doesn't make it OK, and it still sucks to have people picking you apart. But hopefully it gives some context.

So, here's what you have to do: You can be honest and be like, "I don't like when you come at my body." They may be resistant and do it anyway, but now they're doing it knowing that it makes you uncomfortable. After years of just taking her mother's fatphobic comments, Susana finally told her, "Stop commenting on my weight. It hurts my feelings." It took several tries, but eventually her mother respected her boundaries.

You can also just not feed into it and say, "Yep. I love my hair like this. It looks cute, Nana." If you are confident (even if you're faking it) it will let them know that they aren't going to be able to control you on this issue. (And if you are not confident yet, head back over to the body chapter so you can get there.) You might also need to find some allies in some of your aunties or cousins who can help you out. Let them know that this makes you uncomfortable and ask them to stand up for you or back you up when you stand up for yourself.

A NOTE ON BAD BLACK MOTHERS

We can't do a chapter on the family without saying something about the Black mother. Bad Black mothers are common media tropes where Black women are blamed for the all the problems in the Black family and in the Black community. Black mothers are always the problem to be blamed and corrected and can't win for losing. Working mothers are rebuked for not being home with their children. Welfare mothers are demonized for not working. Single mothers are blamed for not providing a good father figure for their children. Young mothers are belittled for having unplanned pregnancies. Queer mothers are rejected for having nontraditional families.

A lot of this stems from a really troubling report published in 1965 called the *Moynihan Report*, which essentially argued that poor Black women who were the heads of households were emasculating potential male partners and destroying their children's future opportunities. This wasn't just a regular report—this was a government document, so it influenced policymakers to view Black women as schemers and cheats who unfairly demand assistance from the system. Instead of examining the structural barriers in our communities, it concluded that all of our issues stem from the Black family, and the Black mother specifically.

But this view was present long before the *Moynihan Report*. In a 1904 pamphlet entitled *Experiences of the Race Problem: By a Southern White Woman*, the author claims of Black women, "They are the greatest menace possible to the moral life of any community where they live. And they are evidently the chief instruments of the degradation of the men of their own race. When a man's mother, wife, and daughters are all immoral women, there is no room in his fallen nature for the aspirations of honor and virtue . . . I cannot imagine such a creation as a virtuous black woman."

We still see this type of vitriol and blame of Black mothers today, even within the Black community. Whenever the baby mother of an uber-rich celebrity requests more child support, she is attacked and called a "gold-digger." We still see people asking "Is he raised by a single mother?" when young people adopt troubling behavior in response to the structural racism in their 'hoods. We still share way more stories highlighting "bad Black mothers" in the news than we do about "bad Black fathers." We have internalized these views of Black mothers, and we need to work to resist them. We need to be conscious of when we see these tropes at play and not perpetuate them.

Definitely don't do it with your own mama. Black women are not to blame for the structural issues that plague the Black community. Black women should not be demonized for making a family in the face of the structural barriers that make it difficult to build and maintain two-parent households. Black mothers deserve support for the raising of their children. Remember that.

BOOED UP

*H*ave you ever been trying to kick it to somebody you really liked and one of your friends or one of their friends just kept hanging around, being an unwelcome third wheel? When it comes to dating, patriarchy is like that unwanted third wheel, hanging around uninvited, cracking awkward and inappropriate jokes, and making it hard to get to know the person you are interested in.

When you feel unsure about who should make the first move and who should follow whom first on Insta, it's the patriarchy. When you find yourself playing games about how long you should wait before responding to your future bae's texts or DMs—definitely the patriarchy. When you're out here second-guessing whether you should show how smart or accomplished you are to a love interest, especially if that love interest is a boy . . . you guessed it. It's the patriarchy. (OK, this last one really pisses us off. #MasculinitySoFragile. And toxic and fragile masculinity go hand and hand. Far too many cis males are socialized to dominate their partners, especially when those partners are more femme-presenting. But if you beat them on a test or get the right answer to a question or do a better job impressing your boss at work, dudes' faces be on the floor, all cracked up because they got bested by a girl. Like we said: masculinity is so damn fragile. It's wack, and it deserves to be called out.)

Patriarchy turns what should be fun and exhilarating into a whole kind of power play. And whenever we are talking about power under patriarchy, there are winners and losers. There are folks who get chosen and folks who get rejected. So, the whole scenario becomes about not being selected rather than about figuring out whether this is really somebody worth your time and affection.

Relationships shouldn't be about playing power games. Healthy love—feminist love—is rooted in the idea that everybody has agency, that everybody's desires and needs matter and should be heard and taken seriously. The goal is not to get the upper hand but to be able to have the freedom to ask for what you want in terms of affection and affirmation. Frankly, we're not sure how feminism got a reputation for being anti-love. We love love. As long as it's rooted in mutual consent and pleasure, spread love! Don't get it twisted.

This is why we're so doggedly like, fuck the patriarchy (#FTP). It messes every-thing up, especially the good stuff. Patriarchy, not feminism, is the thing that messes up good love connections.

Of course, all of this sounds good until it's time to actually try to make a love connection with someone you're really into and your feminist principles keep getting in your way. We're not going to pull any punches here. Dating may not be easy for you. Especially if you are a thinking girl or a skeptic or prone to challenge things or outspoken. Those things make dating tough. This is especially true if you choose to date boys, because unfortunately guys don't live in a world where they are required to show up for girls in a dependable way. Nonfeminist dating wants you to shrink yourself. Be less assertive, be more submissive, be less disagreeable, push back less, ask fewer questions—be smaller. But we're not doing that! We want you to bring all of you to the table, and if homie's not into it, oh fucking well! (We also wholeheartedly believe that at some point in your life you're going to encounter someone who will like you for having those exact things. It just may take you a little longer.)

Also, we really don't want you to think being booed up is the ultimate goal in life. Feminism allows you to imagine a more expansive and more robust life that's not centered on bagging somebody. Too often we narrate the completion of our lives as that we meet our soul mate and get married and have kids and that's when our life really starts. Feminism helped us to reimagine a different way to live our lives. We realized that hobbies and friends were important and fulfilling life goals. We also realized that even if we wanted to have a lifelong partner, we could also have "situationships" and lovers along the way. Not all of our relationships are meant to be marriages.

This is not to say that we do not care about love and sex and pleasure and romance. But sis, it's a mixed bag. There's no guarantee it will go well right away. And we just don't think your whole life should be about getting a partner. Being the person you want to be—a person you like—is actually exciting and something to look forward to.

But although dating while feminist can be a bit tricky, it's not impossible and can be enjoyable. We have a few suggestions that might help you make a love connection and disrupt the patriarchy at the same time.

Remember, girls can shoot their shots too

We don't subscribe to patriarchal notions that masculine people are the ones who have to take the risky first step. If you're a femme or nonbinary person and you see somebody cute, who says you have to wait on them to notice you first?

We know this is easier said than done. What if they reject you, laugh in your face, or gossip about you? The horror. Most folks we know (us included) would rather do almost anything else than face up to the possibility of rejection.

Here's something you should know: We all have these little baby haters inside of us keeping us from taking risks. Your baby hater will have you imagining the worst-case scenario and keeping you from taking that leap! But what-ifs can go both ways! What if they say yes?! What if they are relieved that you talked to them because they were too nervous or afraid to talk to you? We know it's cliché, but it's also true: No risk, no reward!

What if you're trying to holler at another girl? How do you make your intentions clear? You're probably going to have to just be upfront that you like the person because, depending on your gender presentation, your flirting may just come across as you being friendly. You may be trying to push up by saving a seat on the bus and bringing her candy, and she may think you are trying to be her new BFF. Honesty may be your only option here.

But, and this is a big but, you need to make sure that it is safe for you to holler at another girl. Is this person also out? If not, can you safely and emotionally date someone who is not openly queer? You need to establish some boundaries for yourself so you do not unwillingly become some straight girl's "experiment." Are you in a super-conservative environment where openly dating could lead to bullying and harassment? The answer to these questions may change your ability to date right now, and you might need to wait. And trust, you won't be alone. There are plenty of girls whose parents won't allow them to date for a variety of reasons. So you'll just have to keep thinking about what kind of partner you want and what kind of partner you want to be until the day comes.

Date without an end in mind

We really have to work hard to undo the idea that marriage is the ultimate goal for women and the place where all relationships need to lead. A bit of big-sister advice here—stop imagining the wedding after the first date! We can't tell you how many imaginary aisles we've dragged prospective baes down in our heads only to later realize that homie had some trash ways that would make them a horrible life partner. (We blame the fact that we were partly socialized by the old Disney princesses, whose stories legit ended once they went down the aisle.)

When you date without an end in mind, you can really see the relationship for the beauty (or ugliness) that is in the moment. You can evaluate this person for what you like about them right now and not about their potential to hold you down as a spouse. Not to say that you may not one day need to have a conversation about where your relationship is going, but that does not need to happen now. You have a whole life to live.

Let go of gender roles

Another way to kick the patriarchy out of your dating life is to let go of gender roles. (This applies to everyone but is particularly important in hetero dating.) You know, those so-called rules of dating that say things like the girl should fix the plates and the dude should pay for dinner. Men should be providers and women should be nurturers. Boys should be the ones to ask girls out and girls should play hard to get. It's enough to make your head spin.

We've got to let that go and instead structure our relationships around our own strengths and abilities. Maybe you pay for the dates over the summer because you make more with your summer job, and other times you split down the middle. Maybe he fixes the plates at his family functions and you fix the plates at your family function (or everyone makes their own damn plates since you know what you want to eat). Maybe you do the prom-posal because you know you're the real romantic in the relationship. All of that is up to you and is really no one else's business.

Not sure how to let this go? Talk to your friends in same-sex relationships and see how they make these decisions. This is not to say that queer couples are free from expectations that a person who is masculine-presenting behaves like a boy and a feminine-presenting person behaves in ways we associate with a girl. But they often do a better job of pushing past those expectations. In our experience, they tend to have figured out ways to be in a relationship with each other that relies on figuring out what works best for them and not what society has deemed appropriate based on gender.

Be OK with rejection

Look, no one likes rejection. It is an unfortunate part of life. However, the sooner you learn not to make it about you, the better off you'll be. The truth is, sometimes people just aren't that into you. Maybe they were digging you at first and after a while they started acting funny. Maybe they were honest and told you that they weren't feeling you anymore. That hurts, but it's OK. We've learned along the way that there are two kinds of people in the world: those who are really digging you and can't get enough of you, and those who really aren't feeling you like that.

The problem is, we spend so much time trying to convince the ones who aren't checking for us that they should that we end up neglecting those who do. And let's be real, there are some people you don't really rock with. Sometimes it's because of something they did, but sometimes it's just something about them that you just aren't into. Imagine that they had plenty of friends who liked being around them, but they spent their time and energy trying to change who they are just to make you like them. Wouldn't that seem strange? So if the girl you were kicking it with all last month is not feeling you anymore, that's cool. It happens. (Hopefully, she kept it real with you and didn't just leave you wondering what happened.) Do *not* internalize this and take it personally. Sometimes it's really not you, it's her. And it's not that there's anything wrong with her either, you're just not her flavor. But trust us, you're the exact flavor someone else is craving.

Consider polyamory or an open relationship

We think letting go of the idea that relationships have to be between only two people boots the patriarchy out of relationships.

OK. Hear us out on this one. Polyamory (from the Greek *poly,* "many, several," and the Latin *amor,* "love") is the practice of having intimate relationships with more than one partner, *with the informed consent of everyone involved.* The informed consent is the key here—this isn't just one person stepping out and cheating.

Are you saying, *Whaaat?* We get that. It took us a minute to wrap our heads around this idea too. But monogamy is not the only approach one can take to dating and love. Some people like to focus all their attention on one person at a time, and that's fine. Other people like the idea that no one person can or should be expected to meet all their needs for companionship, partnership, and sex. So nonmonogamous folks pursue a range of romantic connections simultaneously, including being in open relationships or being polyamorous.

One of the things polyamory helps us do is combat the jealousy that often arises in relationships. Jealousy is not love, but we often confuse it with love because the feelings are so intense. But you don't own anybody. It's the patriarchy that tries to convince us that we do. Jealousy, and the controlling behaviors that usually accompany it, is all about mitigating risks because you are afraid that you'll get hurt. You're trying to control the outcome. But the truth is, there is a risk of getting hurt with dating no matter what you do. In polyamory, you have to deal with the fact that your special person may have another special person. You have to focus on what is special about you and your special person and not worry about what happens outside of your relationship.

The challenge with being poly is that some folks are merely trying to play you and are using the language of polyamory to gaslight you. And to be very clear: dating lots of people and refusing to commit isn't the same thing as being poly. Poly folks have to be highly ethical, transparent, and honest. And everyone in the arrangement has to agree. No one can be in the dark about what's really going on.

Being in an honest, transparent multiperson relationship is known as practicing ethical nonmonogamy. This can be fun, it can keep things interesting, and it can remove the pressure on any one person to try to fulfill all your romantic needs. Willow Smith currently practices polyamory, and she's living her best life.

Honesty and transparency takes cheating off the table and allows you to see if you even really like this person. Chanel remembers being absolutely obsessed with whether someone was cheating on her, so much so that she ignored all the ways that a person was an asshole, mean, or just incompatible. She evaluated the "goodness" of a dude based on whether or not he cheated. When she decided to give an open relationship a try, it took the distraction of fidelity off the table and allowed her to really focus on things like ensuring that they were building strong communication skills, establishing honesty and trust, and being kind to each other.

Even if being poly isn't for you, you should still live by the practice that the person you are dating should not be your only significant relationship. Chanel also remembers getting so wrapped up in her first boyfriend that she stopped doing things with her friends in order to hang out with him. She would spend hours on the phone with him, and when her friends would beep in, she would make empty promises to call them back. Slowly but surely, he became her best friend. She told him all her secrets, they had their own little inside jokes, had mutual hobbies, and spent all their free time together. But then he cheated on her and she had no one to turn to. All those friends she couldn't make time for eventually moved on with their lives. So there she was, looking like Boo-Boo the Fool. Not because homeboy cheated (his disloyalty was not her fault), but because she allowed herself to be all-consumed in that relationship at the expense of all others. She vowed that she would never do that again. She applies the concept of many loves to her friendships so she always remembers that her relationship with bae isn't the only important relationship in her life.

Use your crew

Friends play an important role in dating while feminist. They can be your wingpeople—asking someone for their number on your behalf or kicking it with homeboy's friends while you flirt. When your baby hater is telling you to sit down, your crew is there to encourage you to shoot your shot and help you strategize a plan to make it clear that you want to be more than their homegirl. They are your cheering section when you finally land the date and your support group if things go left.

Dating is hard, so there is no place for bad friends who demean you, or tell you you're out of someone's league, or holler at your crush. Your crew has to be consistently bigging you up. Anything less just won't do.

SO HOW DOES A FEMINIST ACTUALLY SHOOT HER SHOT?

OK, so now that you're on board with the idea that you can date while feminist, the question is how do you actually kick it to the person who makes you imagine vacays, joint selfies, and double dates with the crew?

Flirting

Real talk, though: flirting is hard if it doesn't come naturally to you. All the flirting tips in magazines and on blogs run the risk of having you out there looking like nobody loves you or you're constipated. We don't want that. We want you to win.

One approach, if you're feeling very bold and looking good on some particular day, is to just be direct. Brittney's line when she makes the first move is, "Hey you're cute. And I'm dope. You should call me." Then she slides the digits.

Confidence is key. This approach has netted a few dates. The con is that the potential for in-your-face rejection is high. The key to managing this is that you have to know the sentence itself is true. They're cute (or smart, or sexy, or intriguing, or, or, or . . .) and you are dope. If they can't get with that, their loss! Keep it moving.

If the direct approach feels too intimidating, another idea might be to just get the conversation going and see where it goes. One of Chanel's friends used to ask, "Do I know you from Baltimore?" even though she'd never seen the person a day in her life. The point of the question was to get a conversation started. If they said they were indeed from Baltimore, then she would follow up and ask what part. If they said they were not, then she would follow up with asking where they were from. The con with this approach is that it may not be obvious that you are trying to holler and you may still end up having to let the person know your intentions.

Slide into those DMs, sis

We already told you girls can shoot their shots too. So if it really goes down in the DMs, this could be a good approach. The benefit of this approach is that you don't have to see the person's face when you holler. And depending on the platform, you don't even have to know if they ever read what you sent. The big con is that if the person is an ass, they can screen shot you and put you on blast. That's not the business. But DMs can work.

Get you a wingperson

If you wanna go analog and old-school, how about getting you a trusty, reliable wingperson who will act as a go-between? The benefit of this approach is that your wingperson can run interference for you, they can report back what future bae's face looked like when they told them you liked them, and they can also let you know if there are any red flags to be on the lookout for. The con of this is that you could get into a he/she/they-said scenario, and things could get messy. It could also backfire and your crush could end up trying to holler at your homegirl (a true homegirl would curb that and let you know). The key to using a wingperson is that after they make the initial intro, they have to use an efficient exit strategy and *skrrrrt*. You don't want them all up in the mix like that because, like we said about the third wheel, too many people can ruin the vibe.

———

OK. That's it, my dears. There really are no rules except:

✓ Go for the things you want.

✓ Always use honesty, care, and compassion when dealing with people.

✓ Consent, consent, consent.

✓ And when you bet on yourself, you always win.

We want you to be an advocate for yourself and what you want in your love life. Partnerships and relationships are a long game, and when you bet on yourself, you always win in the end. You might not get it at fifteen, but you deserve what you want.

A NOTE ON GASLIGHTING

There are all kinds of messed-up things that happen in relationships, but we want to take a minute to talk about gaslighting, because it is particularly pernicious.

Gaslighting is a form of psychological abuse in which false information is presented with the intent of making you think you're bugging out. Someone might deny some shit you clearly remember them doing ("I never told you you were ugly") or constantly tell you you're overreacting. They may tell you that they're "just joking" or something that you are concerned about "isn't a big deal." They may also ask you for evidence and proof of the things that you bring up. As a result, you'll find yourself feeling confused and crazy and constantly wondering if you're being too sensitive. You end up questioning yourself and your reality.

Don't fall for the okey doke. How you feel matters, and no one can argue against that. If your interactions with this person leave you feeling horrible or second-guessing yourself, that's reason enough to be out.

Fuck if I have proof of anything. I shouldn't feel like you're being unfaithful or you don't really like me or you're being disrespectful. If I'm feeling like that and you're requiring me to prove it—I'm out.

You don't need anyone else to validate your reality. Patriarchy believes that you need a photo, video, a confession, or to catch someone in the act for it to be valid. Feminism believes that your gut and your intuition matter. Trust your gut. It's been holding you down your whole life.

THE BECHDEL TEST

Very early on, we start getting these messages that we should risk it all—our friendships, we mean—for the chance to get close to a romantic partner. That is incredibly basic, fucked-up, and wrong.

Did you know that in Hollywood, there is something called the Bechdel test? For a film to pass the Bechdel test, two women have to be onscreen, talking to each other about something other than a man.

First of all, let's point out how low of a standard this is. So if two women talk to each other in a film about the weather, it would pass. Are you unimpressed? We're unimpressed. And yet, across time there have been such a paltry number of films that imagine a world where women talk to teach other about something other than men that a test had to be invented to capture the few that have done it. Do you know how few movies pass the test? Well, only 44 of the 89 films that have won Best Picture at the Oscars pass, so there's that.

This fact tells us something about how deeply our culture under-values relationships between and among women. It also tells us how heteronormative our culture is. Most movies work from the premise that all women are straight and all women value the men in their lives more than they value other women, men, or nonbinary people with whom they have relationships. This is a heteronormative premise, one that places straightness at the center of every woman's life.

LET'S TALK ABOUT SEX, BABY

You know we wouldn't write a book about crushing girlhood without talking about sex. We wouldn't leave you hanging like that. We remember being your age, and chances are, if you have not had sex yet, you are probably thinking about it. And as a young feminist, you are also probably wondering what feminist sex looks like and if that's even a thing.

It is! Imagine a world where people didn't care about when girls lost their virginity or the number of sex partners they have had. Imagine being able to openly admit that you want to have sex and unapologetically dictating the kind of sex you want to have—free of judgment and shame. Imagine women and girls making our own choices about our bodies. A world where our bodies truly belonging to us. Imagine our sex lives being our business and all sex being consensual, pleasurable, and guilt-free. Imagine that.

Well, that's what feminist sex is like. But unfortunately, the patriarchy won't let us be great. So much of our sexual experience as women and girls is injected with patriarchal ideas of what sex should be like. The patriarchy wants us to believe that we should be ashamed of our sexual feelings and perpetuates a virgin/whore dichotomy.

This dichotomy is as old as time (we're talking Virgin Mary old). The idea is that women can fit neatly into one of two categories: we are either innocent, well-behaved good girls, or we are morally inept, promiscuous bad girls. By putting us in these limited boxes, any violence and mistreatment we experience becomes our own fault. If we just acted, dressed, or spoke "right," then bad things wouldn't happen to us. It tells us that we ourselves can undo centuries of patriarchy and toxic masculinity by behaving as "good" girls. (This is total BS. Women and girls get sexually assaulted in sweatpants and hoodies.) This is how we end up with people asking "What was she wearing?" and engaging in other slut-shaming behaviors. It creates external measures of how we should behave, such as men declaring, "We want a lady in the streets and a freak in the sheets." The truth is we are complicated people who don't fit neatly into anyone's boxes. This is why we love those shirts that say "Coretta and Cardi" because they are saying stop pitting us against each other. We are full, complete humans, and you don't get to define us.

The patriarchy also wants us to believe that we and our bodies exist solely for the pleasure and conquest of men. That we are unspeaking objects without needs, desires, and thoughts. This is sexual objectification: the act of treating a person solely as an object of sexual desire without regard for their humanity. For women, it turns us into commodities to be bought and sold. We see this in music videos and magazines that show women as body parts with no faces and no names. When we are reduced to objects, we cannot have our own sexual desires or seek pleasure.

The patriarchy also tells us that we do not have authority over our own lives and our own bodies. We are taught that our parents (namely our fathers), our husbands, our doctors, and our legislators know what's best for our lives. *Bodily autonomy* is the right to self-governance over one's own body without external influence or coercion. Our feminism is one that believes we must #TrustWomen. We are not vessels or incubators or objects. We say bump all that! We are smart and capable, and we reject control over our bodies by any entity other than ourselves. You should memorize that.

We believe that sexual freedom is a super-important part of our freedom as women and girls. Our feminism is *sex positive*. That means that we believe that consensual sex is a natural and healthy part of human life that should not be shamed or stigmatized. We want you to have sex-positive girlhoods filled with bodily autonomy, sexual freedom, and so, so, so much pleasure. We want you to recognize your own desires and take control of your own sexual health. Because we live in a world where sexual assault exists, slut-shaming exists, victim-blaming exists, misogyny and misogynoir exist, and unequal access to reproductive health and justice exist—sex positivity is a must! We wish for you sex that is consensual, pleasureful, honors your bodily autonomy, is as public or private as you want, and is free from patriarchal guilt.

misogynoir: misogyny directed specifically against Black women

In girlhood, this means that you get to choose. And for many of you that may also mean that you are not interested in sex just yet, or you may never be (see "asexuality"). That's perfectly fine too! Sex positivity is not about having sex all day, every day. It's about having control over and defining the terms of your own sexuality.

We didn't have the luxury of being sex positive in our younger days, but we do now, and it is wonderful! So we came up with a list of nine things we now know about sex that we wish we knew then, that would have freed us from patriarchal guilt, valued consent, affirmed our bodily autonomy and sexual agency, and ensured our sex was pleasurable.

WHAT IS CONSENT?

Consent is a mutual agreement between two people to engage in sexual activity. Sex without consent is sexual violence. Period.

A few things to keep in mind when thinking about consent:

- No is definitely not consent. No means no means no.
- The absence of a no is not the presence of a yes. Silence is not consent.
- Consent can be withdrawn at any time. Saying yes today does not mean you're saying yes for every single time. Saying yes on the phone and then changing your mind when you get to the crib is totally fine. Saying yes when it gets started and changing your mind midway through the actual act is also fine.
- Minors cannot consent to sex with grown-ups.
- People who are mentally incapacitated cannot consent to sex.
- If you're drunk or under the influence of drugs, you cannot consent. Think about it like this, if your friend is too drunk to drive, she's clearly too drunk to consent to sex. And there are people who are perpetrators who specifically try to get girls drunk or high for the very purposes of taking advantage of them. This is not consent.

We are well aware that sometimes people like to have sex while they are under the influence of drugs or alcohol. And if this is true for you, we really want you think about why this may be. Why do you feel it's important to be drunk or high to have sex? Are you using substances to lower your inhibitions or anxieties around sex? Did you have a previous sexual experience that was unenjoyable or traumatic and you can't get in the mood without something in your system? It may be time to rethink your relationship between sex and substances so that sex becomes a natural and healthy part of your life.

• If a person removes a condom or pokes holes in it without your consent, that's a form of sexual violence.

NINE THINGS WE WISH WE KNEW: SEX FREE FROM PATRIARCHAL GUILT

We wish we knew that virginity is a BS social construct

Yep. You heard us right. Virginity is made up and doesn't exist.

Is your mind blown right now? All right, we'll walk you through what we mean. The first sign that virginity is some BS is that you cannot measure it. Sure, there's a thing called a hymen that some people believe breaks and bleeds when a vagina is penetrated for the first time. But here's the thing—not every female is born with a hymen. Also, your hymen can break doing a split or riding a bicycle or from a ton of other things. So, evidence of blood on sheets as proof of virginity is pure hogwash. (Also, how do males measure when they lose their virginities? See where we're going here?)

Second, the way we define it makes absolutely no sense and is totally hetero-sexist. Most people define "losing your virginity" as a sexual act in which a penis penetrates a vagina. But that definition totally leaves out queer girls. Are we saying that a girl who has only ever had sex with other girls is a virgin? We think by the sheer fact that they have way more orgasms than straight girls, they would beg to differ. Also, who says queer sex can't be penetrative? And not all girls have vaginas anyway. What if someone has only had anal sex? Are they a virgin?

See? It starts getting complicated to hold on to the idea of virginity when you start asking questions. The idea of virginity also takes away agency from sexual-assault survivors who did not have control over the first time they were penetrated. We stand with the many people who have said that since rape is not sex, these "sexual" experiences do not count. You see why we say virginity is not real?

In fact, the belief that virginity is a real thing has only led to more violence and control against women. The concept of virginity has worked to regulate what we as women and girls do with our bodies. This ends up making us feel like crap about our sexuality and our sexual experiences. It creates a kind of purity culture in which we are taught that if we have sex before marriage, we are damaged goods and our bodies are impure. Then you end up with weird-AF "purity balls" and with girls pledging their virginities to their fathers. You also end up with fathers like T.I., closely monitoring their daughter's virginity by asking doctors to do hymen checks, with an intact hymen being a testament of how "good" of a girl she is. (When the World Health Organization had to come out and address a statement a rapper made, you know it was ridiculous.)

Look, we are not trying to say that any act where genitalia and bodily fluids is involved is considered sexual intercourse. And we definitely are not discouraging you from marking your own first time. But we are saying that since virginity is total BS, you get to make it up for yourself. Maybe for you, your first time will be marked by the first sexual encounter you had where you felt safe, comfortable, empowered, and free from patriarchal guilt and shame.

NOTE TO ADULTS

Our kids' sex lives are none of our business. (Of course, the exception to this is if they are being groomed, molested, or raped.)

This is an idea that may be hard for us to wrap our heads around, because when we were coming up there was a lot of emphasis on what we were doing with our bodies. However, we really should be trying to do this differently. Repeat after us: "My teenager's sex life is none of my business. It is my job to help them make good and healthy decisions and trust that I've done a good job."

If it helps, you can go ahead and make the choice to assume they are having sex and govern yourself accordingly. Their intact virginities should not be a badge of honor for us as parents. And it's an odd thing to measure our parenting success against. Our jobs should be providing a judgment-free place for them to receive medically sound, evidence-based information so that they can make the best decisions for themselves.

Also, what happens after they begin having sex? Should we stop talking to our kids about sex? There are so many other things, including bodily autonomy, consent, trust, safety, that begin long before and well after they have sex for the first time.

We wish we cared more about our edges than our body counts

Now that we're grown, we promise you, this is the most irrelevant thing. Literally. No fully functioning adult cares about how many partners you've had. Meanwhile, we care quite a lot about the state of our edges right now and wish we would have known more about protecting them. We wish the women in our families would have asked, "Are those microbraids tight on your hairline?" instead of saying dumb stuff like "Your hips spreading. I bet you're having sex." We wish we talked about how to massage our hairlines instead of who was the biggest ho in school. So now there are a lot of grown women walking around with low body counts and thin-ass edges we can't get back. SMH.

Here's the thing: body counts are just another way of the patriarchy policing our sexualities anyway. It is rooted in slut-shaming—denigrating girls for being seen as sexually loose, and there's a huge double standard at play. If you are boy then you are seen as "the man" for having a lot of sexual partners, but we get judged and demonized. How Sway?

One way it does this is by making stuff up about how vaginas actually work. We are told that too much penetration can lead to them being worn out and stretched out. But the truth of the matter is, vaginas are designed to bounce back. They can literally push out whole babies—so they can handle whatever body parts a dude has. (Also, if you have not taken a mirror and looked at your vulva, now would be a great time to go do that.)

Sometimes people worry about body counts because they are insecure about their ability to please someone who may be more experienced. They fear that they don't have anything new or exciting to bring to the table. If this is someone you care about, you may want to find other ways to affirm their insecurities. (If not, then telling them "that's a you problem" is totally fine).

There are plenty of women who are pushing back against these unfair standards. Slut Walks (protests against rape culture in which women dress in revealing or "sexy" clothing) are a thing all around the country. Radio host Angela Yee makes it a point to declare that "hos be winning" when people try to slut-shame in her presence. And we have women like Rihanna, the City Girls, and Megan Thee Stallion who are owning their sexualities and who don't give a damn about how many people you think they're sleeping with. They're living their best lives.

Sexual partners can give you valuable life lessons and allow you the opportunity to explore your sexuality. And at the end of the day, there are plenty of girls who have been labeled "hos" who are doing just fine in the love department, and many girls who have tried to live up to ideals of purity who struggle to find love. It's a mixed bag, sis, so you might as well listen to yourself and ignore other people's guidelines for what you should be doing with your body.

We do realize this might be easier said than done, and some of you may have been on the receiving end of slut-shaming or even had pictures and videos of you shared around school. We imagine that this is super embarrassing, and even if the people who leaked the pictures are held accountable, it doesn't change the fact that the world knows your business. That sucks and we're sorry this happened to you. (Also, the leaking of your images completely violates consent and, in most states, there are legal actions people can pursue). But you are not the first girl this has happened to, and unfortunately, we doubt you'll be the last. Our advice? Maybe just own it. (Them: *We saw that video of you giving Johnny head.* You: *Let me see. I did my thing right there. Some of my best work.*) Don't try to deny it was you or be ashamed in what you did. Own it and take their power away. Your friends will rock with you regardless, and everyone else will deal.

But what if it's a deep fake and someone edited a video in a way to make it look like you were involved in a sex act that you weren't? That's tough, and deep fakes are a problem in many sectors of society. This is new territory and the technology is moving faster than the law. While we don't know the answer, we do know that this is when you really need a crew that can support you and adults on your team. They can help you figure out what kind of justice you want. Do you want to have your parents pursue legal action? Do you want to enlist the support of a tech person to help reveal all the ways that the video is bogus? Do you want to advocate for information literacy to be included in your school curriculum? Or do you want to just say, "That shit is fake but believe what you want to believe," and move on? A good crew will be there to support you no matter what you choose.

We wish we decided to have sex solely because we wanted it

We want you to have sex because it's a part of your development that you are ready to explore. Period. Not because you are in love. Not because someone is pressuring you. Not because you are afraid that someone is going to break up with you or lose interest in you if you don't.

The patriarchy creates these kinds of "ho hierarchies" that tell us that if we have sex before marriage, doing it for love is better than doing it simply because we want it. That's still perpetuating the virgin/whore stuff by saying good girls do it for love and bad girls do it for pleasure. This further prevents us from being full humans. Also, in a culture obsessed with body counts for both boys and girls, us girls tend to think that doing it for love will protect us from being a notch on someone else's belt and running our numbers up.

The thing about sex is that it involves another person and it is possible that someone can hurt you regardless. They can have sex with you and break up with you the very next day, tell the school about what you did, or just start treating you differently. Sex is a risk. But imagine putting all this on the line and you didn't even really want to do it in the first place. A shame! You have to ask yourself: If we end things a week later am I going to be OK with what I've done? We believe that if it's what you want to do, you can always live with it, no matter the outcome.

You also shouldn't have sex just because all of your friends are doing it. You can celebrate and support their sexual choices without feeling like you have to be doing the same thing. But on the flipside, your friends shouldn't be calling you uptight or pressuring you to have sex either. We want your friendships to be sex-positive spaces that feel supportive of the sex choices you make. Friendships can be a wonderful component of a fulfilling sex life. They can be a place where your share experiences, troubleshoot difficulties, ask awkward "How do I do . . ." questions—and celebrate when you finally bag a shorty you've been eyeing, or finally get the Big O.

We wish we were vocal about our sexual desires and how we wanted them met

When Summer Walker said, "Girls can't never say they want it. Girls can't never say how," we felt that in our souls. Why is it OK for boys to be sexual beings, but we can't communicate our very normal needs for affection and good sex?

It is not strange to have sexual desire. It is totally natural and normal, and a lot of people your age are feeling this way. You are not going to hell for wanting to have sex and wanting it to be good! Your orgasm and your pleasure matter. You can and should be vocal about what you want. And being vocal about the sex you want, both before and during sex, is totally feminist. Think about it: it requires finding your voice, communicating your needs, and it takes cooperation to make it happen. What can be more feminist than that?

We also want to help you set realistic expectations about what good sex is. Sex takes some time to figure out and get right. Not everyone is going to be good at it, and there will be some interactions that work better than others. But you get to figure out how you like it and tell the person you're getting down with what's working for you and what's not. You don't have to just lay there wondering when it's going to be over while the other person is having the time of their lives.

(Tip: If you can't fathom what it looks like to be vocal about what you want, check out Lil' Kim's *Hard Core* album. She unapologetically demanded good sex for herself. But be warned, this album has a Parental Advisory on it. It is definitely called *Hard Core* for a reason.)

Also, let us just say this: sex is not over just because the person with the penis came! Fun fact: While men having sex with women have orgasms 95 percent of the time, women with men only get there 65 percent of the time. However, there is an 86 percent success rate for girl-on-girl sex. Seems like we should be counting how many times the girl comes to mark completion, right?!

We wish we stayed the hell away from anybody who wanted to beat it up

So much of heterosexual sex is rooted in conquest and violence and not in intimacy and care. For boys, getting laid is a perverse rite of passage, and failure to do so indicates a failed masculinity. Sex becomes a key way for boys to access manhood. If that is the standard for boys, then girls must be sexually available. And it isn't just conquest. It is also about domination. They want you to walk away limping so they know they "killed that shit." Some of us like it like that, and if that's you, then that's cool. But the personal is political, so we need to at least question the ways we got to a place where many boys see sex as conquest and that they have to go through our vaginas to become men. For girls of color, this is exacerbated by people trying to add variety to their sex portfolio. Girls of color will hear things like "You're my first Asian," "I always wanted to have sex with a Black girl," or "I heard Latinas are the best at . . ."

We're not blow-up dolls that exist for male pleasure. This is a place where mainstream porn definitely got us effed up. It has everyone thinking that sex looks close to what we see online—the girl is always hot, ready, and waiting. Sex is nothing like porn; we need to be warmed up and ready. We wish we knew this was BS from the jump so that we wouldn't have such skewed notions of what sex was supposed to look like and the roles we were supposed to play.

We wish we knew that even as teenagers, we had a right to bodily autonomy

Bodily autonomy is the right to self-govern our bodies without external influence or coercion. We live in these bodies every day, therefore we should be trusted to know what's best for them.

A part of bodily autonomy is control over our reproductive lives. While access to abortion is a part of that, so is access to safe and affordable birth control and the ability to make informed choices about those things. This is called reproductive justice and is defined by the SisterSong Women of Color Reproductive Justice Collective as the "human right to maintain personal bodily autonomy, have children, not have children, and parent the children we have in safe and sustainable communities." Supreme Court Justice Sandra Day O'Connor said, "The ability of women to participate equally in the economic and social life of the nation has been facilitated by their ability to control their reproductive lives."

People have been trying to legislate our wombs for a really long time. But even if you live in a place where reproductive justice is tricky, you got options, sis. Check your state laws. You may be able talk to your pediatrician or go to a local clinic to explore a range of birth-control possibilities that make sense to you, and your meeting may be confidential. Local clinics also usually sell condoms and dental dams for low prices (which makes it super easy to keep them on deck in case a sucka claims they don't have one and tries to slide through unprotected. Our health matters, and we must demand people take the proper precautions when it comes to us. No glove, no love.) There are apps that allow you to track the days you are ovulating, and you can avoid sex or take extra precautions during those days. Even if you're not ready to be sexually active or if you're only planning to be in queer relationships (lesbian sex can still transmit STIs, and some girls have penises), learn what's going on in your body and how to keep it safe. You are your own best advocate.

Periods are also a part of reproductive justice. Many of us grow up in cultures that tell us that our periods are dirty and something we should be ashamed about and talk about in secret. Women and girls across the globe experience period-related pain, shame, and ostracization and face barriers to accessing basic menstrual-health information and supplies. Some are excluded from functions like cooking, visiting religious spaces, or even sleeping in the home. Women in prisons struggle to get menstrual products, and women have even been fired for bleeding through their clothes at work. Some trans men and gender nonbinary people experience safety concerns and a lack of access to menstruation products. We believe that period products should be free and easily accessible.

We wish we knew we could say no even if we said yes before

Look, you don't have to continue having sex just because you started. For many of us, the first time was just kind of meh. If your experiences have been similar or you're just not that into it or you don't think it's worth the risks, it's OK to have the attitude of "been there, done that" and move on. Even if your next boo knows that you had sex before and tries to use that to pressure you into having sex with them, you can still be like, "Nah, I'm good." You don't owe anyone your body. And we're not talking about a strict declaration of celibacy or even suggesting that you put a time stamp on how long you're going to abstain. We are simply saying that you can just be like, "That's not something I want to do again for a while." You have the rest of your life to be sexually active. There's no rush.

We wish we had sex with no games involved

With boys being encouraged to "game" girls into sex and girls being socialized to deny their sexual desires, it's a wonder how anyone is having sex at all. Some boys' interactions with us may not be sexual assault or rape, but they are coercive tactics and they still feel icky. These include things like begging you over and over again; making it feel like you owe them (because you did it before, because you love them, and so on); threatening to have sex with someone else; making you feel sorry for them by talking about what your abstaining means for them (for example, "blue balls"); calling you names like "a tease" and claiming that you led them on; reacting with sadness, anger, or resentment; or even telling you that they love you as a tactic to manipulate you into having sex. We need a world where girls can comfortably explore their sexualities so that we can say yes when we want it, and at the same time, boys respect our nos when we don't.

We're also really concerned about the way that boys are told that they *need* sex. This is a really reductive version of boyhood and manhood. They are not animals who can only bend to their primal urges. They are fully functioning humans with a range of interests and desires that are not all about sex, and they are capable of informed, responsible choices.

We wish we realized that the best kind of feminist sex is with ourselves

We fundamentally believe that in a world that tells women and girls that we should hate our bodies and deny ourselves pleasure, we girls need to take time to turn ourselves on and admire our own bodies.

Some of you may have been told that self-pleasure in the form of masturbation is weird, gross, unnecessary, or should be a secret. But have you realized that boys seem to talk about masturbation as a normal, ordinary thing? We need to be equally unapologetic. Plus, exploring what works for you is big FTP energy and brings together all the components of sex positivity. Where else does it get to be all about you, your body, and your pleasure? And when you know how to please yourself, you don't ever have to depend on anyone else for your own orgasm. ("All the women who independent, throw your hands up at me.")

But masturbation also enriches sex with a partner, because when you know how to please yourself, you'll feel much more in control and confident when telling someone how to please you. You can give clear and precise instructions of exactly where you'd like them to go.

As if you needed any other reasons to play with yourself, there are some pretty cool health benefits to masturbation as well. It helps reduce stress and anxiety, prevents urinary tract infections, and helps with cramps during your period, just to name a few.

We think self-pleasure is so important, we put together a little playlist of songs that celebrate exploring your body and sexuality. Enjoy!

SELF-LOVE
PLAYLIST

Tweet, "OOPS (OH MY)"

Kelly Rowland, "FEELIN ME RIGHT NOW"

Carly Rae Jepsen, "PARTY FOR ONE"

Lady Gaga, "DANCIN' IN CIRCLES"

Rihanna, "SEX WITH ME"

Macy Gray, "B.O.B."

Pink, "FINGERS"

Charli XCX, "BODY OF MY OWN"

FKA twigs, "KICKS"

Cyndi Lauper, "SHE BOP"

T-Boz, ft. Richie Rich, "TOUCH MYSELF"

Nicki Minaj, "FEELING MYSELF"

Britney Spears, "TOUCH OF MY HANDS"

Toni Braxton, "YOU'RE MAKIN' ME HIGH"

Lizzo, "SCUSE ME"

SEXUAL HEALTH RESOURCES

Planned Parenthood (plannedparenthood.org)

Clue (helloclue.com)

Girlshealth.gov

AMAZE (amaze.org)

Center for Young Women's Health (youngwomenshealth.org)

Scarleteen (scarleteen.com)

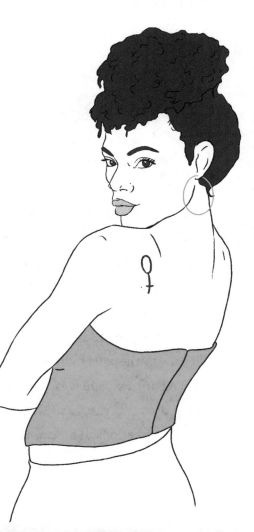

AIN'T NOBODY MESSIN' WITH THE CLIQUE

*H*ave you ever noticed what happens as a new woman rapper hits the scene? It seems like the comparisons with other women rappers follows immediately. We watched it happen with Foxy Brown and Lil' Kim. We saw it later between Nicki Minaj and Cardi B, and people definitely tried with Megan Thee Stallion and the City Girls. But when it comes to men, we don't see those same kinds of comparisons. Sure, there are conversations about who's the greatest, but it is far more likely they will get placed into a three kings category (see J. Cole, Kendrick, and Drake), while there can only be one woman on the throne. They love to see us at one another's neck.

By now, you all should know what this is. That's right, it's the patriarchy. Part of the way the patriarchy works is by dividing women and femmes over petty ish and pitting us against each other. This isn't just a hip-hop thing. Media perpetuates this myth through TV shows like *The Bachelor* that show women competing for the affections of a man. Women politicians are consistently pitted against each other, with endless comparisons about which woman we like best. And you probably see this in your school as people rank the prettiest, smartest, and/or coolest girls in the class.

And the unfortunate thing is, it works. Many women and girls proudly declare, "I don't hang with other girls," saying that girls are too catty and petty for their liking. Mind you, we have never heard a boy say he doesn't hang with other dudes because they can't be trusted. Yet, for many girls, it still remains a badge of honor to be "one of the boys." They prefer the company of boys who they think don't gossip, backstab, or do drama. (Let us just say, this is unequivocally false. Don't believe the hype. Trust us, they do all of these things.) And look, we are not saying that girls are not capable of doing you dirty. They are. But why do we dismiss all girls because of what one or two have done? We never hear boys saying that about other guys!

But there is a way out of believing the hype. The first thing you have to do is believe in the value of forming solid friendships with other women. Everybody of every gender needs good homies, but if you're a girl, this is especially true for you. One of the most basic ways you can challenge cultural norms is by being a woman who decides to ride for other women by investing time and energy in cultivating solid friendships. Every woman and girl who aspires to be a feminist cracks this code of girl friendship, usually before they do anything else. Because what kind of a world is it if feminists don't like other women?! We can't have that.

So, let us tell you about the value of homegirls:

BUILT-IN CHEER SQUAD Seriously. Your girls, if you've got good ones, will be your own personal cheer squad. Who but your homegirls will hype you with a "Yassss, bish! You rocking that skirt! That hair is fiyah!" Your girls got your back if a fight is about to pop off, but they also know how to keep it from getting to that level ('cause we need way less violence in the world and, sis, you got goals, so keep it tight). And even if your friends don't have all the right words, check for the folks who show up for the stuff that matters to you.

BATTLING THE -ISMS Battling white supremacism, sexism, capitalism, homophobia, transphobia, and ableism already causes enormous pressure. If you go to (or went to) predominantly white schools, you get both these subtle and overt messages that you aren't good enough or don't belong there. If your school is more racially and ethnically diverse, then sometimes folks police how you do your Blackness or the authenticity of your Latinidad. It's anxiety-producing and some version of it happens at every stage of life. The thing that makes it all better though is having homies to look to with the "You see this bullshit?" face or to help you forget the heaviness of it all.

YOUR HOMEGIRLS ARE LIKE THE BEST KIND OF SOUL MATES You get all the benefits of romantic relationships and sisterhood without the complications of

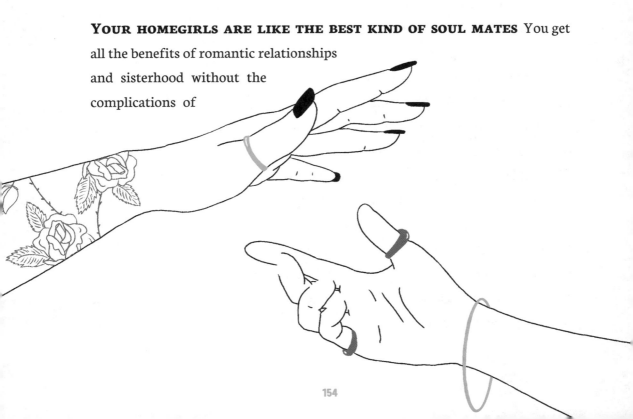

wanting to have sex with someone or the obligations of being actually related to them. These are also places where you can share your secrets and dreams.

You ain't gotta share everything. It's perfectly fine to keep some stuff to yourself. But sometimes, Black and Brown girls suffer and struggle because we carry too much, don't trust easily, and don't know when and how to let folks in. Our homegirls give us a soft place to land.

FRIENDSHIP IS THE PLACE WHERE YOU CAN ASK THOSE DIFFICULT, NON-PC QUESTIONS You can't just go up to any Black girl and touch her hair or any Muslim and ask about how they pray. But in friendship, there is a trust and a safety that allows for these kinds of conversations. You know this person loves you and cares for you and is not trying to make your difference feel wrong. In friendships there is trust, love, and bonds that can withstand the curiosity.

THEY ARE A SHOULDER TO CRY ON Our homegirls have loved us fiercely, even when we did not love ourselves. They have been there with us through heartbreaks and first kisses. They encourage us and challenge us to grow. We are all better women because of the homegirls we have had to walk with us along the way.

Brittney often talks about her love for the Baby-Sitters Club book series (and now Netflix show), about a diverse group of friends who started a local babysitting business. She loved the adventures they got to go on and the way that all the skills and talents of each and every girl were valued in the group. Most important, she loved the way they always had each other's backs. The characters taught her something important about friendship: that good friends celebrate our best parts, hold our tough parts, and are a safe haven for us to love and be loved. Doesn't everybody need that? Of course we do.

FRIENDSHIP WOES ————————————————

Friendships, like all relationships, can go awry. Even great friendships can experience hitches, pauses, and outright breakups

So what happens when friendships go wrong? Here are some common friendship woes and our advice on how to handle your friendship troubles crunk feminist-style:

I've been getting kind of friendly with this girl in my gym class. But I don't trust people easily, and I find myself pushing away. How do I know when I should trust someone enough to make them a new friend?
There's nothing wrong with being cautious about who you give the friendship title to. A friend isn't just someone you have fun with, but someone you rely on for advice and who you may tell your secrets to. We totally get wanting to take your time with that choice. If you are worried about what it looks like to trust someone, observe them from afar. You don't have to make fast friends. But see how they do with other people. If someone is always gossiping about somebody else's business, then that's a person you know will tell *your* business. They may be fun to party with, but keep your deepest, darkest thoughts and desires to yourself.

Between homework, baseball practice, church activities, my weekend job, and college apps, I really don't have time for friends. They'll understand, right?
Part of the challenge of building lasting friendships is actually devoting time or energy to getting to know another person. This means you have to be genuinely curious about what is going on with them and intentional about finding and nurturing your points of connection. Former First Lady Michelle Obama has

written that "friendships between women, as women will tell you, are built of a thousand small kindnesses . . . swapped back and forth and over again."

This has been true for many of our friendships. We have to disrupt the idea of busyness. It just fuels an individualistic idea that teaches us what we produce is more important than our relationships. You *have* to make time for friendships. They hold value. It's fine if things are a little bit hectic right now and you need to grind hard for the next week, but sometime soon, schedule time with your homegirls to check in on them. These are the people who are going to hold you down if life throws you a curve ball, and they're the ones who'll celebrate those wins with you. You have to nurture those relationships and treat them as just as important as the other things. This doesn't mean they should take all of your time, but you have to make time for your friendships. Those are the things that sustain you.

TIP: Try creating a relationship tracker and set a goal for how often you want to talk to your friend. For example, maybe you want to talk to your friend once a week. Every time you talk to them, give yourself a gold sticker (because who doesn't love stickers?). This is a fun way to make sure you keep in touch with the people you care about.

Sometimes I feel like I have to choose between my boyfriend and my friends. I want to spend time with my homegirls, but me and my boyfriend don't see each other much, and I want to spend all my friend time with him. Shouldn't my relationship with my bae be the priority? It's a great question. First, life is hard and people are complicated. In that same vein, no one relationship can meet your every need. This is another lie that the patriarchy tells us. It tells us that your relationship with your bae should supersede every other relationship you have. As feminists, we don't believe that. It's not that romantic partners don't matter. They absolutely do, and they are often the people we choose to build families with. But friends can be family too. In fact, we prefer it that way.

Me and my best friend have been friends since we were in preschool. However, lately we're really not as close as we used to be. What should I do about this?

Sometimes friendships naturally dissolve over time. For instance, a friend can move away and even though there are text and video chats, it can be difficult to maintain friendships over long distances. Sometimes the shift in friends, interests, and life circumstances just leads to a natural evolution.

Brittney's Story

From elementary to middle school, my bestie was a white girl named Amanda. We loved hanging out, having sleepovers, playing together at school, and talking on the phone during long summer breaks away from each other. In seventh grade, though, Amanda's friend group became more white and mine became more Black. In our small Southern town, I knew that racially integrated dating wasn't a thing that would be broadly accepted, and our friend groups followed our dating patterns. We both sort of sensed we were building new bonds and naturally began to part ways. We still had love for each other and all the memories, but we both needed different things. Sometimes that happens and that's cool.

If this seems to be a natural thing that is happening and you're both on the same page about it, then just let it rock. If, however, you sense that something may have happened to cause this new distance, check in with your friend and ask if everything is cool. You can just say, "Hey. I've noticed a bit of a shift between us. We good?" It may be possible to mend the friendship.

Also, even though people don't really talk about what it's like to lose a friend, we think it's totally normal for us to mourn the end of friendship. We do it when a romantic relationship ends. Just like when you break up with ex-bae, you miss talking to your friend on the phone and the memories you shared. There may be a bit of a mourning period over the realization that the friendship has ended, and that's OK. Give yourself the same space you would if it were your boo. Friendships matter too.

OMG! My bestie has a new bestie and I can't deal. Help!

Sometimes conflicts can happen because a new friend is introduced to the crew and it changes the dynamics.

Perhaps before you act out, you should talk to the friend or somebody you trust who gives good advice about what you're feeling. When you really vibe with a friend, and you don't vibe with their other friends, it can be off-putting and a little disconcerting. You can doubt yourself, your place, and your value. Or, conversely, you might just be being a little territorial and cliquish, wanting to keep all the friend magic to yourself. Friendships have to be mutual and reciprocal, period. They can't be about ownership. As people of color, we know about this country's sordid history with owning people, and we have to root out that impulse in ourselves.

We're not saying you're trying to turn your bestie into a slave, but sometimes our desire for exclusive access is about control. But the dopest thing about friendships is, they free us up to be our best selves. Every relationship we have should do this for us in some way. But here's the thing, sis: we don't own people. People don't belong to us.

We used to think you could only have one bestie. For some people that works. But for others, they have a bestie from middle school, a bestie from the old neighborhood, a bestie from summer camp, a bestie from college, and so on.

You could also have a friend who is best for going to parties with, one who is best to share your secrets with, and one who makes the best study partner. We say, the more the merrier. This notion that there can be only one is patriarchy and white supremacy at its finest, and we have to just say no to that idea.

Brittney's Story

I will be the first to admit that I haven't always navigated this terrain well. In eighth grade, my bestie started being really cool with this other chick we knew from gym class. They would be in the corner kiki-ing about the new girl's crush, and I was irritated. This was my bestie—we had agreed explicitly that we were BFFs, and I felt like she was violating the arrangement. So I had a stank attitude toward the new girl and basically went out of my way to ignore her and not include her.

At some point, my mother (as mothers do) advised me of the error of my ways, and I felt guilty about how I had been acting. So first I talked to my bestie. She set up a little convo at the end of gym class, and I apologized to the new girl for how I had treated her. I said, "I'm sorry that I have been mean and rude. I was feeling a little insecure about your friendship with _____, and I acted out because of it. I hope you can forgive me, and if you're willing, I'd like to try to be friends." She listened calmly and said, "I thank you for your apology, but I don't wanna be friends."

That stung. But she was well within her rights. I had been raggedy to her, after all. But because I apologized and cleaned up my behavior, we never had any issue ever again.

So, my friend did something so low-down and dirty that I don't know if I can forgive her. She completely broke girl code. What should I do?

Look: sometimes a friend, somebody you care deeply for, can legit do you dirty. They might betray a confidence, they might fail to show up when you really need them, they might date or sleep with your person. Shit happens and it sucks.

If you really feel like this person cares about you, tell them how you feel, and communicate to them what you need them to do to make it better. And when they follow your process, stick to what you said. If, however, a person does something you didn't see coming and they aren't sufficiently apologetic, then maintain your boundaries, remember that you have the right to be treated well, and understand that this conflict has exposed you to what might be an uncomfortable truth about who that person is. Armed with that knowledge, you should reevaluate if it's a healthy friendship for you.

Being a good feminist and loving other women doesn't mean you don't get to have good boundaries or that you have to put up with behavior that makes you feel bad about yourself. Being a feminist is about loving yourself enough to know your worth.

If a friendship breakup happens, it's OK to mourn the loss of that friendship and its good parts. It's great to reflect on any lessons you learned from the interaction. And it's important to remind yourself that you are worthy of having great friendships.

Chanel's Story

In high school, my best friend started dating my boyfriend behind my back. To make matters worse, neither one of them told me that they caught feelings for each other and I had to find out from someone else. Serious girl-code violations, for sure. We instantly stopped being friends and turned into bitter enemies, constantly trying to one-up the other when it came to this boy. The beef culminated over a year later with a physical fight at a gas station. (Clearly not one of my shining moments and a huge feminist no-no.) But we were eventually able to see that we were both being ridiculous for letting a boy come between us as friends.

Looking back, we definitely could have handled this differently. She should have been honest with me and communicated her feelings, and I should have talked to her first when I found out. We might not have been able to reconcile, but it definitely would have prevented it from getting to the point of a physical altercation. (And we both should have been done with a dude that would pit two friends against each other. Trifling!) I am happy to say that this story has a happy ending. A few weeks after that fight, we ended up making up and becoming friends again. And we are still friends today, texting weekly, going to each other's special events, and making it a point to see each other whenever we're home.

Brittney's Story

That bestie that I was so pressed and territorial about? She ended up being a terrible friend. She'd talk about me behind my back, always take everybody else's side in an argument, and go around treating me like I was her uncool sidekick. (I admit she was cooler, but that isn't the point.)

I saw all these things about her, but I put up with the behavior for years because I didn't think she would treat me better, and I didn't think I would find other friends. We were two Black girls stuck together in a predominantly white environment and I felt we needed to stick together, even when something she did or said made me go home and cry every day.

It took me a long time, but I finally stopped holding on so tightly. I realized that I was a good friend to her and I deserved good friendship back. So I let the friendship dissolve in its own good time, and the more I did that, the more that people who I actually liked and vibed with showed up.

Friendship is not about uniformity. You and your crew don't all have to look alike. It's wonderful when we have friends from our culture and racial background whom we don't have to explain our shared norms and customs to. However, sometimes our communities can place some pretty rigid boxes around what it means to be a member of that group. And if you do something that does not fit into the box, then you are seen as not Black enough, not Indian enough, not Latinx enough, etc.

If you can't find members of a group that you can rock with, it's perfectly fine to expand your horizons. Do you bond with other girls who also love to play *Fortnite*? Then add some gamer friends to your village. Do you get along better with the elders in your church? Then add some intergenerationality to your village. Diversity of opinion, life experience, and approaches to solving problems are things that make friendship exciting and keep it interesting.

Part of the way you make friends is that you have to look outside of your comfort zone. Go find the other misfits. Give yourself permission to do that. Look outside of the group of girls you think are supposed to be your friends. Don't worry about trying to impress them.

Brittney's Story

At the end of eighth grade, my terrible bestie went on a class trip with her honors section. I was worried that I would be alone at school for the better part of a week without my crew. But it turned out to be one of the best moments of middle school. I spent those three days with other kids in my class and had a great time. I didn't realize that there were people I could be friends with all around me until I was forced to shift my angle of vision. Then I learned that I was cool in my own way, good at adapting in social situations, and fun to be around. I never felt any of those things with #TerribleBestie.

Susana's Story

Growing up, it was often hard for me to make friends. I wore dorky glasses and was chubby and nerdy. In some ways, I didn't fit the ideal of a Jamaican American girl in my 'hood, someone I saw as fierce, fearless, well dressed, and didn't take any ish from anybody.

At that point I didn't realize that, one, everybody's faking it until they make it, even the cool girls; and, two, there are so many ways to be a Black girl. While I always had Black and Brown friends, it just didn't come easy. By the time I got to college, I had come into my own in many ways. I fully embraced my nerdiness, was learning to love my body, and rejected the idea that I had something to prove to be likeable. That's when I met my BFF, Eesha. We had a lot in common, like being nerds, loving books, and having working-class immigrant parents. We had also both grown up in the North and moved to the South as teens.

A big difference, though, is that she's South Asian and I'm Black. Mostly our shared love for Jane Austen, carbs, and feminism has brought us closer over the years, but we definitely have different experiences. There are cultural differences, since our people are from different continents, have different religions, and have different native tongues. But some differences have little to do with our cultures. Even though I'm the daughter of two immigrants, folks are usually surprised to find that out about me, while folks are always asking Eesha where she's "really from" or asking about her ethnicity. On the other hand, the experiences I've had being followed around stores or the scary encounters I've had with police are different from hers. But because she's my BFF, I've got her back and she's got mine. We can keep it 100 with each other with no fear of judgment and without worrying that our feelings or experiences will be downplayed. Although we are very different in some ways, my bestie's unconditional love and sisterhood has been a cornerstone of my life.

What if I don't have friends and struggle making new ones?

We want to keep it real with you, and the truth is, you're going to have to slog through some of this girlhood stuff. It sucks, but we promise that it does get better.

First, consider how you treat other people. Are you open, friendly, and engaging? (You can be friendly even if you're shy.) Do you hold grudges? Do you know how to apologize if you screw up? We aren't asking you these questions so that you can beat yourself up. We've all done some not-so-friendly things. But we do want to make sure you self-reflect and course-correct if you are engaging in these behaviors.

If it is not the case that you are being unfriendly, then more than likely the issue is not you. It's your environment. There may be some real limits in your community that may make it difficult to find your people. You're not just feeling like the people around you don't get you; they probably don't. But that doesn't mean that there is anything wrong with you. Your community is out there waiting for you to find it.

You might be like Brittney and find your people at debate camp. Or like Susana and find your crew in college. Or like Chanel, who always had separate groups of friends who got pieces of her, but found her flock when she went to grad school and finally found a group of nerds who also "liked to do hood-rat stuff with their friends." You're going to have to create a plan to get to the places where your people may be.

And don't be afraid to make friends online. There are plenty of people who have become really close with people they have met through their blogs or

Instagram pages. (DMs aren't just for shooting your shot with someone you want to date.) This is an easy way to find people who you already know share your interests and get you. Just make sure to do some form of background checking (hop on a video chat, check out the mutuals, or hop on the phone) to make sure your new friend is real and you aren't being catfished.

If going online is not an option for you, you may have to get comfortable with having fictional friends. You're going to have to fall in love with characters in books, television shows, and movies and take comfort in the friendships you see between the pages.

But trust us. You'll get older and there will be people who appreciate the things that made other people reject you. And that time will be here before you know it.

Susana's Story

When I was in high school I was hella shy and found it hard to make friends. I had moved from the Northeast to south Florida in the seventh grade and was still getting my footing. Even though I went to the same high school as my middle school crew, we didn't really have any classes together and could only hang out at lunchtime. Over time, most of us drifted apart and I was very bummed out about it. Plus, my school was ginormous, with over 3,000 students. Lowkey I felt like a lonely ant marching through the hallways with my heavy-ass bookbag.

But after a while I was like, I can't live like this. I made a conscious effort to take a chance, be vulnerable, and make new friends in my classes. Sometimes it worked and sometimes it didn't. But putting myself out there was like building a muscle, I got stronger every time. I made friends in chorus and creative writing— folks I still am friends with today! But I'd be lying if I said I had some kind of super-dope social life. Besides having a super-strict immigrant mom who clocked all my movements, I spent a lot of time at home doing homework and chores, listening to music, reading, and playing video games by myself. I really learned to love my own company while cherishing the fun times I had with my small group of friends.

MOVIES ABOUT GIRL
FRIENDSHIPS

SET IT OFF

WAITING TO EXHALE

TROOP ZERO

B.A.P.S.

THE COLOR PURPLE

GIRLS TRIP

HIDDEN FIGURES

SKATE KITCHEN

MOSQUITA Y MARI

CLUELESS

A LEAGUE OF THEIR OWN

GIRLHOOD

THE CRAFT

BEACHES

LADY BIRD

THE JOY LUCK CLUB

THELMA & LOUISE

FRANCES HA

TROOP BEVERLY HILLS

CROSSROADS

THE BABY-SITTERS CLUB

JOHN TUCKER MUST DIE

HARRIET THE SPY

BIRDS OF PREY

BOOKSMART

MYSTIC PIZZA

ME WITHOUT YOU

THE FEMINIST FRIENDSHIP CODE _____

We want you to have BFFs. No, not best friends forever, but "Better Feminist Friendships." What is the difference between a regular friendship between girls and a feminist friendship? Is that even a thing? Yep! It most certainly is. And feminist friendships are freaking awesome. They are friendships that are governed by respect and mutuality and end up making you a better person. We lead with love. We prioritize loving, affirming, and fun interactions with each other above all else. But they don't just happen. We, the feminists, declare:

ARTICLE 1: **WE WILL NOT LET THE PATRIARCHY GOVERN OUR FRIEND-SHIPS.** This is the most important rule and the one the others fall under. Under no circumstances do you allow the messed-up ideas that say that women must be in competition with one another, be solely focused on romantic relationships, or be overly concerned with what we and other girls look like to govern your friendships. Memorize this and hold it dear to your heart.

ARTICLE 2: **WE WILL NOT FIGHT OVER A BAE.** (You can have them, sis.) Look, we get it. It's natural to feel like fighting when you find out that someone betrayed your trust. Maybe they told you they didn't have a girlfriend and you found out they did. Maybe you found out they've been messing with someone behind your back after promising to be faithful. Maybe you found out that the person they were creeping with was your bestie. *Ooooh.* That's a violation for sure. Or imagine you find out that he has a crush on your bestie. Let it go. Walk away. They are not worth it. Also, what if your BFF is your real soul mate and you blew the friendship for some cornball who doesn't have the decency to keep it 100?

ARTICLE 3: WE WILL NOT ENGAGE IN SHADY, BACKSTABBING BEHAVIOR. This one is simple. We don't betray our friends. We don't sleep with their baes, encourage them to talk about other people and secretly have that person on three-way, or talk shit about them behind their back. So many petty games that people play. We support one another and don't let other people talk trash about them in our presence. You can certainly let people vent about the thing a friend did that upset you. But we draw the line at nastiness, name-calling, and dehumanizing language. Period.

ARTICLE 4: WE WILL LET OUR HOMEGIRLS DEFINE THEMSELVES FOR THEMSELVES. It's not our job to tell other people how they feel or how they should identify. If a friend says something upset her, it is not your job to make her feel like her feelings are not valid. Even if it's something that would not have offended us, we affirm her feelings and make sure she knows they are valid. If our friend says she loves other women, we don't ask her if she's sure or try to dissuade her. We congratulate her bravery and ask her about her crushes. And most important, if our friend says she is a girl, then she's a gotdamn girl. This is a *sisterhood* not a *cis*-terhood. There is no homophobia or transphobia allowed. All are welcome.

ARTICLE 5: WE WILL BE OUR FRIENDS' MIRRORS WHEN THEY CANNOT SEE THEMSELVES. Friends do not make friends feel bad about their looks. Friends do not make friends feel ashamed of their unique gifts and abilities. Friends do not let friends beat themselves up about not reaching arbitrary goals or accomplishments. We tell our friends they are beautiful, even when they feel like they are not. We build them up. We shine a light on their value and their worth. When we say, "All our bitches bad," we aren't talking about something as frivolous as their looks. We're talking about their dope and unique personality, skills, and gifts they bring the world. It is our job to show them when they cannot see.

ARTICLE 6: **WE WILL BE A SAFE SPACE FOR OUR FRIENDS.** A place where they can be vulnerable and share secrets we will never tell. A place where they can talk about their fears, wants, and desires. A place where they can share family drama, trouble with relationships, and new crushes.

Everyone needs a soft place to land. In a feminist friendship, we honor these spaces and commit to keeping our friend's secrets even if we have a falling-out. Even if they tell our secrets. We do not betray this bond. (Now, of course, if a friend tells you they are being harmed, they are going to harm themselves or someone else, or they are the victim of sexual abuse, this rule becomes null and void. You need to tell someone safe for the very reason that you love your friend and do not want her to be harmed or do something that will ruin her future. You can deal with that the fallout later.)

ARTICLE 7: WE WILL HOLD EACH OTHER ACCOUNTABLE TO BEING THE BEST VERSION OF OURSELVES. We want to share with you Brittney's concept of the "Homegirl Intervention" as a way for you to structure your friendship ethics.

Homegirl intervention is when your homegirl lovingly snatches your coat tails to keep you from being raggedy in these streets. Homegirl interventions say: You need to read more. You need to be nice. You need to watch your tone. You need to own your shit. Someone who calls you in rather than calls you out with love. Sis, that ain't it. Sis, we better than this. Sis, Black Jesus didn't die for this.

How do you know when it's a homegirl intervention and not just someone being nasty?

You know a homegirl intervention by how it makes you feel when it's over. Our homegirl interventions have always felt loving and gentle, even when there were things that were hard to hear. You might feel challenged, and it might sting a little bit. Who likes to be told that they're doing too much? But you want friends to love you enough to tell you when you're wrong and to lovingly correct you by saying, "I'm invested in you and I know you can do better." And because your homegirl is invested in your growth and not your embarrassment, homegirl interventions are also only done in private, even if you show your asses in public.

On the flip side, when it's a mean-girl thing, there is a bite to it and it has a tendency to make you feel terrible. These kinds of interactions leave you wondering if the point is to humiliate you or throw you under the bus. You don't leave that interaction feeling lovingly pushed to be your best self. You feel horrible.

A homegirl intervention is a promise to not let you be raggedy. A true friendship says, "I got you, and in your hard moments, I'll be there."

Article 8: **We will have difficult conversations when an offense occurs.** We promise to listen when we have hurt our friend. We promise to apologize (none of this "I'm sorry, but" bullshit).

Use dream hampton's Anatomy of an Apology for guidance:

I'm sorry.

Here's my understanding of how I hurt you . . .

I will never do this again.

Feminist friendships also promise not to let issues fester when we are upset. We will be brave and tell our friends that we are hurt and what we need to be OK. We address the harm, discuss it, and work to solve it. If these efforts fail, that is OK. We know we tried.

Article 9: **We will honor and respect each other's boundaries.** There are so many places where our boundaries as women and girls are not respected. Our friendships should not be one of them. If our friend hates to be told to calm down, then we try our best to not tell them that. If our friend goes to bed at ten p.m., then we don't call them past that time for nonemergency situations. If our friend needs some alone time every day, then we are going to make sure that our girls' trip has quiet time built in so she can have a good time.

Article 10: **We will be committed to building and maintaining antiviolent friendships.** Feminist friendships are nonviolent and non-manipulative.

Look, we grew up in areas where physically fighting was a logical and normalized way to handle conflicts. Someone did something you didn't like, and it was handled with fists when the school bell rang. We get it. Sometimes you want to beat the shit out of somebody. But we can't just run around beating people up because we don't like something that they did.

But let us also say this: There are other, nonphysical ways to engage in violent behavior. We see this in manipulation, gaslighting, and passive aggression. Frequently, we observe that toxic white femininity functions in this way. It is at the intersection of whiteness and patriarchy that we see a particular form of gaslighting where people do things to you and make you feel like you're crazy when you confront them. It hurts when this happens, and it makes friendship so hard.

Physical and nonphysical violence are two sides of the same coin. Both are violent and harmful behavior that we need to quit. We off that. No more riding to her house to fight her and her crew. No more spreading nasty rumors around school. No more bullying-type behavior. That is *not* feminist, and we are going to decide to do better. You actually can just turn it off and decide to be different. Do it. Commit to building loving and affirming relationships and stepping away if/when your friendships become toxic. Commit to unlearning harmful conflict-management strategies and learning how to deal with conflict in healthy and sustainable ways. Learn to recognize toxic relationships and walk away. Learn to recognize your own toxic behaviors and correct them.

ARTICLE 11: **WE WILL NOT HAVE POSSESSIVE FRIENDSHIPS.** It is fine to have a best friend, but you know you can have more than one bestie, right? You can have a best school friend, best neighborhood friend, a best church friend. Best childhood friend. Best college friend. Your best friend can have other best friends. You can have a whole friend village. The idea that we need to have rigid hierarchies of friendships is rooted in capitalist patriarchy. This is not a competition. Love is expansive. We offer you the concept of polyamory to structure your friendships.

Also, there are friends and then there are crews. It's cool to have one or two friends, but it's also dope to have a crew of friends. Crews are like these superpower friendships that are über-diverse and give you everything you need. As Public Enemy rapper Chuck D once said, crews have a kind of protective effect: "The only way that you exist within that mold [of the 'hood] is that you have to put together a 'posse' or a team to be able to penetrate that structure, that block, that strong as steel structure that no [one] individual can break."

Our crews have been our saving graces and give us a team of people who have our backs and support different areas of our life.

This is the code. May we stick to this like white on rice. May we be always open and ready to adhere to its principles and hold our friends to the same standards. And if we have trouble adhering to these virtues, may we be reflective and kind as we try and try again.

4

FIGHT THE POWER

CLASSY, BOUGIE, RATCHET

Our feminism is rooted in a critique and an analysis of class. We believe that without a real class consciousness, we can't ever get to a place where we smash the patriarchy once and for all. That's because even if we created a society where men and women hold equal power, we would still have a system in which people are divided by their economic status, where the more money you have, the better your position.

class: the system of dividing people into groups based on perceived social or economic status.

Here is a quick checklist to help you reflect on some of the ways that class influences your life:

- ☐ I have my own room and do not share a room with a sibling
- ☐ I have more than fifty books in my home

☐ I have a parent who is unemployed, but by choice

☐ I have attended private school or summer camp

☐ My parents or guardians attended college

☐ I do not rely primarily on public transportation

☐ My family takes vacations out of our hometown

☐ I have never been embarrassed or ashamed about my clothes

☐ I have never had to move because my family could not afford the rent

☐ My parents or I have inherited, or expect to inherit, money or property

☐ My parents will pay for me to go to college

☐ No one in my immediate family has ever been on welfare

☐ I have never felt that an opportunity was closed to me because I did not know how to dress, speak, or act

☐ I have never lived anywhere that did not feel safe

If you checked a lot of boxes, then that means that you experience class privilege. Privilege is unearned advantage and immunity granted and available to a particular group of people. That means that it's not based on effort, work, skill, or struggle.

People often struggle with the "unearned" part of privilege, so let's think about it like this: Your mom may have busted her ass to become a surgeon and worked incredibly hard to get to where she is. But the fact that we as a society value doctors over grocery-store workers has nothing to do with the effort that she put in. This is not about hard work, but the work that we have decided is valuable.

Having class privilege also means that you have freedom from particular forms of discrimination, and that you have access to "social capital" (relationships to and connections with people with influence or power), even if you choose not to use it.

If you did not check many of the boxes, that means that you experience class oppression. Class oppression is the systemic marginalization and denial of access to resources based on membership in a lower social class. The legal system, educational system, public policy, and media all systematically disadvantage poor people.

Let's take, for example, when schools had to go online due to COVID-19. What if you did not have a computer, or if you had only one computer in the house to share between you and your siblings who all had online learning? Or maybe you had a computer but did not have access to the Internet. Perhaps you figured out a way to use a local parking lot for free Wi-Fi, but you have a harder road to success than a student who has their own laptop and desk in their room to access lessons. It also means that you have access to fewer resources like money, healthcare, and knowledge of how to navigate systems of privilege.

It's important to understand our positioning in the class system. It is also important that we do not hold any guilt around our privilege or shame about our oppression. You cannot help your privilege. That's the whole point—it is unearned. You also did nothing to earn your disadvantage. There's no reason to feel bad about it. There are so many contributions (ideas, culture, ways of being) that poor people have made to this country and the world that you can and should be proud of. The important thing is that we learn how it structures our lives and commit ourselves to a feminism that seeks to eradicate class-based oppression.

THE MYTHS ─────────────────────────────────

Part of what makes it so difficult for us to tackle classism is that we have been fed so many myths about class. We, as a society, hold some pretty ugly stereotypes about poor people.

MYTH 1: YOUR CLASS STATUS IS A REFLECTION OF YOUR WORK ETHIC AND MORALS As a society, we often hear it said that poor people are lazy and irresponsible and that if they just worked harder, they could be successful. But can you really say a single mother who works two jobs, one at a diner and another cleaning rooms in a hotel, is working less hard than the CEO of a company? Can you say someone working fifty hours a week in a factory is working less hard than an NBA player?

The truth is, it has nothing to do with how hard people work. Poverty and wealth are often generational. People pass poverty on to their kids, who in turn pass it on to their kids. Its super hard to break the cycle of poverty. And if your great-grandparents were wealthy, you are most likely going to be wealthy too. This is because your ancestors were able to pass down property, money, and investments that helped their families for generations to come. This stuff is structural. Hard work isn't really the issue here.

MYTH 2: POOR PEOPLE DON'T KNOW HOW TO SPEND THEIR MONEY This is another really nasty myth that gets perpetuated about poor people. We believe that poor people are irresponsible and "if they didn't spend their money on Jordans or Fendi bags, they wouldn't be broke."

The problem with this is that it ignores the many factors that are actually contributing to poverty, like access to good schools and affordable healthcare. It also ignores the extremely low wages that most Americans make and the huge gaps between rich and poor. Those Jordans ain't got nothing on discriminatory housing policies that created the 'hoods in the first place! Focusing on an individual's material purchases puts too much pressure on people and lets society, fuck-ass policies, and greedy people in power off the hook.

Also, why can't poor people have nice things? As poet Nikki Giovanni asked, "Why is it that poor kids have to wear Keds and everybody else can wear Michael Jordans? . . . [That] every kid has a leather jacket, but the Black kids have to have cloth?" Gotdamn! We gotta be poor *and* miserable?

MYTH 3: POOR PEOPLE LIVE OFF HANDOUTS WHILE UPPER-CLASS PEOPLE EARN EVERYTHING THEY RECEIVE The handouts thing is an interesting one. We place a lot of emphasis on food stamps and Section 8 housing as government programs that are designed to help people who need assistance with food and housing. But are we just going to act like tax breaks for married couples, subsidies for farmers, and tax cuts for corporations are not government assistance programs? Hmmm. How many times have huge Fortune 500 companies been bailed out to the tune of a few billion or trillion dollars? But we upset about welfare programs that cost less than 2 percent of the gross domestic product?

Keep your head on a swivel. This is a distraction technique.

MYTH 4: PEOPLE ARE POOR BECAUSE OF SINGLE MOTHERS AND ABSENT FATHERS First of all, you should probably be wary of anything that puts the blame on Black mothers. There's a long history of using them as the scapegoat for social ills. So, when it comes to poverty, the theory goes that single Black mothers aren't able to adequately raise their children in a way to make them contributing citizens to our country. Do you know how many of the people we label #Goals are the product of single mothers?

The truth is, that's just another way to demonize women who bear the brunt and the burden of poverty. And they also throw out this thing about absent fathers as if there aren't plenty of two-parent households that are still in poverty. Like we said, this shit is structural!

THE REALITY

The myths are so pervasive because it is so much easier to blame individuals than it is to blame what seem like invisible pieces of a system that keeps people rich and poor.

It is also difficult because some of us who grew up poor have internalized these messages. Poor people themselves often justify classism and believe that the class hierarchy is fair. They even sometimes exhibit hostility and blame toward other poor people: *We* be the main ones telling people how they need to use their tax returns to start new businesses because of *our* belief that we, too, can make it if we just work hard enough. Look, we want you to work hard and dream big. We want you to have nice things and achieve all of your goals. But we don't want you shaming poor people in your climb to the top.

Those of us who have privilege find it difficult to face that privilege. We resist the idea that the things we have are a result of anything other than our hard work. But again, you didn't do anything to earn your privilege—no more than someone did anything to earn their disadvantage. If you've never really had to think about the way your money and access to other resources influences what you can and can't do in the world, that's because your privilege has meant you didn't have to. Again, we are not really talking about individuals. What we are talking about is a system that privileges certain people over others.

But if we are going to build an inclusive girlhood, we are going to have to be united on this front. We have to take class seriously. We want to make room for a girlhood that rejects classist stereotypes and works to build a world in which all humans can live with dignity.

And the first thing we need to do is reject that BS "American dream." The American dream is the belief that anyone, no matter what class they were born into, can work hard and be successful. It is the rags-to-riches story that says that people can pull themselves up by their bootstraps.

It is complete and utter BS. And it hasn't served us well at all. Here's why:

First of all, this dream has been unrealistic for many Americans who for centuries were not allowed to work outside of the home (white women) or who were enslaved (Black people).

It also assumes that we all start on an even playing field. But some of us have to overcome *waaaaay* more obstacles before we get to the finish line. And as we've been saying, while plenty of people work hard, some people's hard work goes a lot further than others because they start further ahead.

Also, the American dream makes it seem as if hard work is an indicator of value. What if you can't work anymore or never could? What if you are disabled, or old, or the industry you worked in no longer exists? Are you simply a burden on society that should be tossed away? We think not!

And don't get us started on the whole notion of individualism that places importance on being self-reliant. What's so wrong with needing other people? We're supposed to be all inspired because a few people from our 'hoods were able to make it out and become millionaires? Like, "If they can make it, so can you." But those people are the exception, not the rule. There are way more people who never make it out. And why do some of us have to live in communities that we need to make it out of? Why can't our communities sustain us?

We have never been fans of the American dream. We've always favored more communal visions. We are driven by a great love for our people, not just ourselves. We dream of healing, teaching, telling stories, and bringing joy to our communities. We're not really into shitting on other people with the things we have. We're into sharing what we have and building relationships on reciprocity.

Crushing girlhood feminist-style means putting our feet on the neck of the American dream and never letting up. We're going to replace self-reliance with "I'm not good if my people not good." We say collectivize everything! We can push back on the idea that we should be doing things alone with an emphasis on cooperation and crew. Our grandmamas raised their children together, sometimes several women under one roof. Our aunties and mamas shared groceries and cooked dinner together. Our sisters formed study groups in college to bust out that super-hard chemistry class. Our friends formed writing groups in graduate school to finish their dissertations. And look at us, writing this book together. We all we got!

SWITCHIN' IT UP

As girls of color, we often live at the border of two cultures—the culture we call our own and the mainstream culture that we work in, go to school in, and interact with on a regular basis. We often make choices about how we're going to show up in each of those spaces. Basically, we switch it up, or decide how we present ourselves based on our goals, and even our safety. We're talking about code-switching, the act of changing the ways you speak, your behavior, appearance, and other factors to better fit into or adapt to different norms.

The thing is, everyone speaks different languages, even if you think you only speak one. You probably speak one way in school, another way at home, another way when you are sliding into the DMs of your future bae, or when you are fighting with a sibling or your BFF. We are all fluent in different tones, registers, and slangs because we belong to a variety of communities. Where it gets troubling is when value is placed on there being a "right" way to be. The idea that there is only one "proper" way to speak, dress, or act is often based in patriarchal, racist, classist, and xenophobic notions. Think about what is held up as the ideal voice, dress code, or behavior. Does it match what you see in your home or community? Probably not. Chances are that if you are a person of color, part of an immigrant community, part of the LGBT+ community, or part of another marginalized community, the standards of your community are not considered ideal.

Sometimes these standards and ideals show up in subtle ways. You look around and realize that no one in positions of leadership in your community or organization speaks like you or dresses like you, so you feel pressure to switch it up in order to succeed. Or maybe the elders in your community hip you to some game and tell you about the things they had to do to be taken seriously.

Other times, these standards are explicitly enforced. For example, there are schools across the country that ban natural hairstyles, such as cornrows, extensions or braids, and locs. This is different from something like school dress codes, which affect everyone who attends the school and are unavoidable unless adults in charge change the rules. These hairstyle rules single out Black folk, who primarily wear them. If there was a rule like this at your school or job, it might make you feel angry, frustrated, or ashamed. Why shouldn't you wear your hair how you want to? Or what about all the drama about bathrooms and trans folk? Creating a rule that forces trans and nonbinary people to use bathrooms based on the gender they were assigned at birth is super invasive and unnecessary, yet there are many places where this happens. You may wonder who this social policing benefits and why things are this way.

This is where code-switching comes into play. One thing we need to know about code-switching is that for people of color it is one of the many tools we have used to survive in a white, supremacist, patriarchal society. Some might argue that being able to switch it up and to speak/dress/act one way at home and another way out in the world is a cool skill to have. True enough, being able to switch it up shows that you can maneuver in a lot of different ways. For some of us, it's a matter of survival. In order to make it through school, work, or just plain old life, we scan our environments and figure out what presentation fits best into what atmosphere. You switch it up to avoid drama, to fit in better, or to stay safe. So if anybody tries to come at you for your ability to code-switch, you can tell them that.

But we also need to remember that there's no shame in choosing not to code-switch and that people choose not to for a variety of reasons. For some people, they cannot code-switch. Code-switching is ultimately about proximity to whiteness and the dominant culture. But proximity to these things is not necessarily a good thing, as it can lead to psychic and physical violence. So being educated in white schools or living in white areas where you have had a lot of experience learning the dominant culture is not better than living in a world in which you have very limited interactions with white people and you spend most of your time entrenched in your own culture.

Other people can code-switch, but they just refuse to do it. They question why we have to code-switch anyway, and what difference it makes if we will be mistreated no matter how much we adopt the ways of the dominant culture. They do their best to keep it 100 at all times. They don't switch up their speech, dress code, or behavior. They may get a lot of heat for not conforming to what is expected of them. Folks might call them out for speaking a language other than English in public, or if they dress in a gender-nonconforming way, or they behave in a way that others deem too loud, bold, or in-your-face. Despite the stigma and the side-eye, these anti-code-switchers may just feel more comfortable not code-switching, regardless of the consequences. You know what? That's 100 percent OK because people get to choose what feels best for them.

But just like we shouldn't knock people who don't choose to code-switch, folks shouldn't knock those who do in fact code-switch. It's all right to be culturally agile and adaptable, just like it's all right to grow up in a community where you've been affirmed that your culture is valuable. For some it's just plain easier, and for others it is a matter of life and death. Ultimately, the blame lies in a system that fails to recognize that there are lots of different ways to be, and not on the marginalized individuals who are caught up in that unfair system.

HOW TO NAVIGATE CODE-SWITCHING

THINK ABOUT HOW YOU FEEL MOST COMFORTABLE Can you be yourself at school, your place of worship, the corner store, and beyond? Why or why not?

CHECK OUT ARTICLES, BOOKS, PODCASTS, VIDEOS, AND FILMS on code-switching, like the *Code Switch* podcast, that can teach you more about social norms and how we conform to or reject them.

CREATE ART—poetry, music, sketches, whatever you like—that helps you to express your feelings about juggling multiple worlds.

TALK TO ADULTS YOU TRUST about whether or not they code-switch and how they feel about it.

THIS IS AMERICA

The famous twentieth-century scholar and writer W. E. B. Du Bois once declared that the problem of the twentieth century was "the color line." We are now in the twenty-first century, and racism, one of America's two original sins, born both of colonizing and decimating Native peoples and stealing and enslaving Africans from their homeland, remains a problem. For the eight years that Barack Obama was president in this century, many Americans convinced themselves that racism was a thing of the past. They used dubious terms like "postracial" to describe that experience. But since America was never "pre-racial," we can't just declare racism over and expect it to be done. That's not how this works.

What, then, does race even mean? Lots of people who fancy themselves super woke and progressive love to declare that "there's only one race—the human race!" (Rolling-eyes emoji!) We have nothing but side-eye for these people, and if you are those people, sisssss—don't be.

Race is a story that people in the eighteenth century—scientists, explorers, lawmakers, and the general white public—began to tell as a way to explain differences in skin color and physical characteristics that they observed in people across the world. There is no genetic marker that makes you Black, white, or Brown, as a race. There are genes that determine skin color, but again, race is the story that a bunch of white people made up in the 1700s to explain what skin color "means." Even though we know race is fictive, by which we mean it's a made-up story, we can't just undo it by putting "race" in scare quotes like another group of super-woke folks like to do.

We can't do that because of *racism*. Racism was an ideology that grew out of the practices of European explorers as they moved around the world, seeking global dominance and empire. They took lands and stole people, and to justify why it was allegedly OK to do this, they touted a narrative of white racial superiority and Black and Indigenous racial inferiority. That ideology, which took people in different racial categories and placed them in a hierarchy, ranking some as smart, safe, and human and others as ignorant, dangerous, and inhuman, had violent consequences around the world.

We cannot just sloganeer our way out of these problems by posting bumper stickers about "one human race," yelling at the people (usually people of color) who point out racism in action to "just stop talking about race!" or even by electing a Black president. The problem is too big for that.

But we can get real, and stay real even when it's uncomfortable, about how racism (and its attendants, white supremacy and anti-Blackness) shape every facet of our daily lives.

That statement makes so many people uncomfortable. It's easier to accuse Black and Brown people of "seeing race everywhere" than to acknowledge that racism is a part of the air we breathe, that it is essential to our system of laws, that our struggles to achieve justice in every generation have everything to do with these systems of human interaction that were invented before any of us even got here.

One of the biggest myths about racism is that "everybody can be racist." We don't agree. Everybody can hold problematic racial attitudes, born of ignorance about groups other than one's own. But systemic racism is rooted in the power to shape and change people's livelihoods and access to justice, based on their race. Only one group of people has that overarching power in this country, and it is white people.

Full stop. No really. Pause. Breathe. Then read on.

White privilege is a real thing, a natural outgrowth of a system that understands white people to be more intelligent, more fundamentally human, and more fundamentally valuable. To be clear, naming systems of white supremacy and the operations of white privilege is not the same thing as saying "all white people are bad." Not all white people are bad. But all white people *are* born with white privilege. And far too many white people refuse to acknowledge this.

If you remember when we talked about intersectionality, then it can offer some insights here. We aren't claiming that white people don't struggle or don't have to work hard for the things they get. Many white folks who grew up poor are especially exasperated by the claim that they have privilege. To them, we say this: It isn't that you didn't struggle. It's that despite all the ways you did struggle, your race didn't make your struggle harder. For Black people and people of color, race and racism invariably make some things, like access to good schools, safe housing, good jobs, and healthy food, harder.

What does this mean, then, for having white friends, dating white people, and navigating predominantly white workplaces and schools?

Here's the thing, y'all. We trust you. The benefit of having a good deep, antiracist, intersectional feminist analysis is that you have everything you need to navigate these hard questions and fucked-up systems with aplomb, agility, and grace.

Now you just have to trust yourselves. If you feel seen, heard, and understood by the people you are choosing to be friends with and date, then those friendships are worth sustaining.

But if you ever have to diminish your race or culture, the music you listen to, or the food you eat as a requirement to fit in, then these probably aren't your people. And even that is complicated. Sometimes you have to put up with some stuff until you can make it to the next phase.

I (Brittney) had mostly white friends in my K–12 years. I was in a predominantly white school system, which was deeply racially stratified. At the time, there weren't many Black kids in my honors, AP, and gifted-and-talented courses. To make it worse, I got bullied a lot by Black students who said I was "acting white" or "talking white." So I chose to be friends with the people who were friends with me. That meant that I had to deal with my white friends' racist parents, and with the insensitive remarks that my white friends sometimes made: "Does your hair feel like a Brillo pad?" "Do Black people see better in the dark?" "Well, Black people do run down the property values when they move into our neighborhood," and my favorite, "You're not like other Black kids." It was shitty on all sides. The Black kids in my school had internalized every lie white supremacy ever told about Black inferiority, and the ones who knew better took out their anger at an unjust system on me. Not cool. The white kids presumed that they were naturally smart, that they deserved to be in honors and AP classes (even when some of them were basic AF and of mediocre intelligence!). They also assumed that being "like them," and "not like the other Black kids," was the proper way to be, that something was wrong with other Black people.

But the realest shit I can say to you about that is that it's easy when you're Black or Brown to build a whole identity on not being like "the other Black kids." It's easy to imbibe and internalize anti-Blackness. It's easy to revel in being the exception, the token among your friends, the one who brings a little pop of color to an all-white friend group, as though you were an accessory to a completed outfit. Don't do it. It's a deal with the devil, sis. Never believe the lies that white supremacy tells about who people of color are.

And don't even believe those lies when people of color are the folks doing the telling. White supremacy is beguiling. Because of how it works as a racial system, so many great resources—schools, coffee shops, entertainment spots—are nicer on the white side of town. And so many of us spend our lives trying to get into as close proximity to all that stuff as we possibly can.

Feminism reminds us that what we are fighting for is justice. We are fighting for everyone to have access to good schools and beautiful parks and nice restaurants. Everyone deserves school trips and extracurriculars, a living wage, and safe neighborhoods. That stuff should not be segregated on the white side of town.

So date whom you want. Be friends with whom you want. But check in with yourself often to ask what those relationships are requiring of you. And even if nobody around you gets you or understands who you are or what you need, make sure that *you* understand. That way, when your people show up—and they will—you will recognize them.

If you have to code-switch a little to make your life work, that's cool. We think of that as a superpower. Maybe you talk all the Black cultural vernacular (slang) or your parents' first language at home and then you switch that stuff off at school or work. That's a resource that people of color have cultivated as a survival mechanism in a world that doesn't value all we bring to the table. So use it to your heart's content.

Code-switch, socialize, be flexible. But don't shrink. You know you are shrinking when folks tell problematic jokes and you consistently say nothing, because you are afraid of what you'll lose. You shrink when you are ashamed to share aspects of your life that you think your friends won't value culturally. You shrink when you do everything to fit in, even when you know it isn't who you are.

Don't shrink. White supremacy wins by asking us to not show up as ourselves in our full humanity and complexity. Don't let it win. Fight the power!

TIPS FOR DEALING WITH YOUR PROBLEMATIC FAVES

Often, friends, relatives, and even randos on social media will challenge our politics with endless problematic commentary. Here are some ways to navigate that.

BE CURIOUS! One of the things that happens often in discussions about race and racism (and queerness and every other *-ism*) is that people fire questions and accusations at you. That immediately puts you on the defensive, and there is no winning from a defensive position. So if someone says, "I think you're being racist for bring up race" or "All lives matter!" ask questions. Why do you think that? Do all lives matter? What about how the world treats Black people suggests that their lives matter? Resist the urge to defend your position, because it is racists who need to defend their position, not you.

SHARE YOUR EXPERIENCES Or what you've read or what you're learning. Begin with phrases like: "In my experience, x is true." Or, "I read about this and it has helped to inform my thinking." Or you can say simply, "I hear you and I think about it differently." And then share your opinion. This approach has the benefit of helping you seem nonjudgmental (though if we're being honest, we do judge racists!). And it will help the other person remain open to dialogue, rather than putting them on the defensive.

DECIDE WHEN TO TEACH AND WHEN NOT TO TEACH You don't owe anyone your intellectual labor. That's what libraries are for! If you feel a person is genuinely curious, open, and responsive to your point of view, and you have time that day, feel free to engage. If, however, they begin to troll, to get belligerent, or to be argumentative, bow out. You don't owe them anything and you have nothing to prove. Moreover, at the end of these discussions, you'll feel tired and upset, and they will feel perfectly fine.

DO NOT TAKE RESPONSIBILITY FOR ANYONE ELSE'S FEELINGS Often when you characterize someone's actions as racist (or homophobic or transphobic), they perceive it as a character attack and begin to cry about hurt feelings. White girls and women are especially prone to invoking "white-girl tears" as a tactic to deflect accountability. In those instances, do not take responsibility for anyone's feelings. You can say: "Racism is painful, and your racism is hurtful." Or you can say, "We are all entitled to our feelings, but I am not responsible for hurting you." Do not accept responsibility! Because you are not to blame. If you don't know what to say, you can also simply disengage, because emotional manipulation is often hard to navigate.

CALL IN RATHER THAN CALL OUT If someone you love or care about says something racist, you can call them in. You can approach them in private or send a text or email flagging the comment that was racist, hurtful, or inappropriate. This way, they have the opportunity to learn and grow without being shamed in public. This is a great approach for your homegirls, your aunt who says inappropriate things about others or even inappropriate things about you or your body, or for those white friends you have who you know are well-meaning but who screwed up this time.

Sometimes powerful people do need to be called out, though, and you should reserve the right to use that tactic in extreme circumstances. But if that's the play, consult with your crew and your allies (or maybe the cool teacher all the kids talk to about everything) before you make that move.

If your teacher says something racist, you can try to address it with them privately, if you think they will be responsive. Otherwise, leave the adulting to the adults. Tell a parent or school administrator what you are experiencing and let them handle it.

I'M COMING OUT

Writer, director, and trans activist Janet Mock has said, "Gender identity is who you go to bed as, versus sexual orientation is who you go to bed with." And just like there are a million ways to live out your gender, there are a ton of ways to experience like, lust, and love.

That's not to say that figuring this stuff out or living your truth is easy. You might be clear about your sexuality. But maybe you have super-duper-strict parents who are all in your business, telling you you're too young to date, much less have sexual feelings. Or maybe you're not super into anyone in particular and you're feeling pressured about liking folks and being booed up. Maybe you're digging your BFF and she's totally oblivious. Or maybe there are grown-ass men on your block trying to holler and you feel grossed-out by their attention. You might like boys. You might like girls. You might kick it with a nonbinary cutie one day and a trans cutie the next. Maybe you're not interested in sex at all and never will be. All of those feelings are perfectly fine, even if there are folks out there in your ear saying otherwise.

Sexuality is all about the type of physical and emotional intimacy you want to have with others. Who we like and who we want to be with romantically and sexually is just one of the many ways we can express ourselves. Sexuality can be complicated or it can be clear-cut and easy. Often, it's a mixture of all of that. Sexuality is a personal experience with political consequences. It shapes how we think about our identity, pleasure, and how we form family and community.

We know that there could be a lot going on as you sort out your feelings. Just know you have the right to feel whatever you're feeling. And you have the right to change your mind. What matters is being true to yourself, honoring your feelings and boundaries, and respecting the feelings and boundaries of others.

Susana's Story

I can tell you this because I know. I've been there. I've been a boy-crazy straight girl, a bi-curious young woman, and a queer grown woman. The journey with my own sexuality has been fun, scary, and amazing.

I had my first real crush in the fifth grade. I'd like a boy here or there, but nothing too serious. I didn't get a lot of play from boys. I was chubby, wore glasses, and couldn't afford cool clothes. Add to the fact that I was super nerdy and a teacher's pet—it was just a recipe for disaster. I got the generic valentines that you write to friends. And for a while I was fine with that. For me, boys had cooties and homegirls were all I needed.

That all changed when I was ten. Lawrence was one of my classmates, a boy I'd known since I was in the second grade. He was smart, so we talked about books together. He also had the cutest little goofy grin. I was totally smitten. Whenever I thought about him I got this dorky look on my face and my bestie would be like, "Oooooooh . . . you have a cruuuuush!" I would deny it, but my face would get all hot and I'd look away all shy. It was a lot of fun. It felt right and nice to be chosen and "special."

A new girl came to our school and was placed in our class. Maya was tall with blondish-brown hair, and she was always dressed to impress. She was a cool friend with a Caribbean immigrant mom like me. She could tell I liked Lawrence and it was fun to giggle about his dimples or what he said in class on our walks home together.

There was a Valentine's Day dance coming up. We were so sure that Lawrence was going to ask me, and one day, as we were grabbing our backpacks and heading home, Lawrence rolled up on us. He looked nervous and kept looking around. I was trembling with anticipation. Then he turned to Maya and blurted out, "Will you go to the dance with me?"

I felt like I was slapped in the face. I wanted to crawl into a hole and die, but I didn't say anything.

Maya looked down at him and then she rolled her eyes and laughed. Then she grabbed me and we walked out arm in arm, leaving Lawrence looking stupid. I felt warm all over and the embarrassment dissipated, replaced by a combination of smug triumph over Lawrence playing himself and a newfound appreciation for Maya. She did have a really cute smile, after all.

Now, I'd be lying if I said my feelings weren't hurt. After all those weeks of flirting for Lawrence just to ask out the tall, pretty, light-skinned girl was, like, beyond basic. The saving grace was that Maya saw that shit happening and nipped it right in the bud! #GirlCode. We never even talked about Lawrence after that. I really appreciated how Maya had my back. And her standing up for me revealed that maybe I was geeked up about the wrong person all along.

That moment taught me a couple of things. First, boys are raggedy and homegirls are everything!

OK, so maybe it's not that simple. Although friends are everything, not all boys are raggedy. But I did internalize Lawrence's rejection. I felt like it said something about me not being cute enough, or being too weird or too nerdy, when in reality Lawrence could like whoever he wanted and his choice didn't mean that I was lesser-than. Still, it took a long time to get over that feeling of judging myself by someone else's standard. It colored how I conceived of my own sexuality. I felt like boys had the upper hand and I was just waiting to be chosen.

I wish I could say that was a moment of true queer awakening, but it wasn't. That would come well over a decade later, when I was good and grown. As a preteen I could not fathom Maya possibly liking me or vice versa. I had completely internalized the heterosexism and homophobia I'd learned from my family and community.

I began feeling super behind the curve in the dating department once I got to middle school. This continued into high school. I wanted to be able to trade stories about boys with my girls. I didn't want to be left out. I even wrote that down in a diary, and don't you know that my mama found it and I got into a whole lot of trouble. She told me I had no business thinking about boys and that I should just be focused on school. I was beyond embarrassed and felt misunderstood.

The thing is that sexuality is a very personal experience. Only you know your feelings and desires. At the same time, sexuality is experienced out in public. Who you love and who loves you affects so many aspects of your life. Right now, there are many places in the world where you can be legally discriminated against because of your sexuality. In the United States, marriage equality has only been the law of the land since 2015!

But even putting the legal stuff aside, there are other ways our sexuality can be policed, judged, and scrutinized—or encouraged, affirmed, and celebrated. Think about who or what are considered "relationship goals" and what is given the side-eye. Often queer sexualities are viewed as suspect or inherently wrong, while heterosexual couplings are bigged up. Or if you're not really that interested in sex or dating, folks might ask, "What's wrong with you?"

Bullying and gatekeeping around sexuality is real. I don't know about you, but there was so much policing of who liked whom and who was dating whom when I was in middle school and high school. If folks weren't checking for you, the assumption was you were gay, and that was the worst thing you could be. When I was thirteen, a friend asked me why I didn't have a boyfriend and wondered aloud if I was gay. Growing up in a conservative Christian household, same-sex attraction was talked about in the same breath as child molestation and bestiality. Queerness was an abomination. I hadn't even come to a realization that I had queer feelings; I just remember being so taken aback at the question that it felt like an accusation. Having already internalized homophobia, it made me interrogate my own behavior and suppress my own desires. Looking back now, I realize my friend might have been grappling with her own feelings and felt the need to project her budding self-hatred onto me.

You, too, might be experiencing that sort of policing. Let me make something absolutely clear: there's nothing wrong with you. Your sexuality is yours, and no one else's business. Those folks have a problem with your perfectly natural feelings and desires. And you do not have to be friends with folks who belittle who you are.

Still, the reality is that sometimes the folks who are checking for who you like are people who are authority figures in your life, like your parents, older siblings, community elders, teachers, and religious leaders. They might be scrutinizing your choices and behaviors because they want to mold you into their idea of what is right. And the truth is that not everyone has the ability to defy cultural or community expectations regarding sex and sexuality. As a young person you may not have the resources or support to do and live exactly as you want—at least, not now. That is totally not your fault; the problem is with your surroundings, not you. When the coast is clear, you can live exactly how you feel. That's not to say it will be easy, but it'll be what's right for you.

When that mess went down with Lawrence, I couldn't put my finger on exactly why I was sad. At the time I felt like I didn't have friends I could share my frustrations with. Everyone seemed to have their shit together, and I was the only unlikable freak who didn't have a bae or couldn't completely sort out my feelings and desires. It wasn't until years later that I realized so many of my friends and classmates were feeling just like me but were afraid to share their true feelings and fears.

So if you're feeling like you're the only one freaked out about your feelings and experiences, whatever they may be, know that you are not alone. Seek out like-minded individuals you can truly be yourself with, whether it is at school, in your community, or online. Having a crew is so important as you figure your ish out!

Brittney's Story

I grew up in a conservative Christian household. This made my attempts to develop a healthy view of my own sexuality feel damn near impossible. We went to church every Sunday. Plus, my stepfather is a pastor. Church is just what we do in my family. Marriage, we were taught, was the only context in which you can have sex. And marriage was also understood as only for heterosexual people.

But like many teens, I had lots of interest in kissing, sex, and figuring out dating. In church, I was taught that having even desirous thoughts outside of marriage was lustful and sinful. It took me many years to undo a lot of this terrible teaching around both my own sexual desire and around the homophobia that I had been taught. In fact, I didn't really begin to figure it out till I was nearly thirty. I hope you figure it out sooner. But here's a little bit of where I landed: First, as both a feminist and a Christian, I don't believe being gay is a sin. I believe that many of us are taught that because we tend to impose our own beliefs on God, and frankly, because many of our Bibles are poor translations of the original language. Second, I think that God made sex good and wants folks who want to have sex to be able to engage in it with both consent and pleasure. (Always, always with consent.) Third, I don't believe sex outside of marriage is a sin. I know. I promise I do. I know what folks think the Bible says, but we've put some books below for you to read and grapple with this for yourself. The bottom line is that in this book we want you to have the tools to engage with your deepest, hardest questions, and come to answers that work for you. I know you or the adults in your life may deeply disagree with what I have said here, but in the end, we all have to come to our own conclusions about our belief systems, whom to share our bodies with, and on what terms. Follow and respect your parents' rules. We aren't trying to get you kicked out the house. And listen to their wisdom. Sex is complicated and messy and wonderful and scary. Let the people you trust help you to figure it out. But your sexuality is your prerogative, no matter what anybody says. And I mean that. On God.

TIPS ON NAVIGATING SEXUALITY

READ, READ, READ More information is always better. There are tons of books, from autobiographies to novels to how-to manuals, that break down all you need to know about sex and sexuality. Follow folks on social media who are affirming and enlightening. Read articles. Just read.

BOUNDARIES, BOUNDARIES, BOUNDARIES Boundaries are a way of loving yourself and honoring people you care about. Think about the kinds of interactions you want to have and that feed your soul and bring you pleasure and joy. If talking to a particular bae makes you feel anxious and terrible—don't talk to them! If kissing another bae has you feeling pressured to do things you're not ready to do—you don't have to do those things! You don't have to make yourself uncomfortable to please others. You don't want to be anyone's experiment. Likewise, it is important to respect other people's boundaries, even if them telling you no makes you feel uncomfortable.

REMEMBER, YOUR PLEASURE MATTERS Create your own pleasure manifesto. Think about the kind of emotional and physical intimacy you want to have and map your way to getting it. Your intimate interactions with others should always center your needs while also being respectful of others.

GAUGE YOUR EMOTIONAL MATURITY Sex is an intimate act, so be sure you're ready to engage with others in that way. That doesn't mean you have to be "in love" to have sex. But it does mean that you have to be ready for the emotions that may come when you are naked with another person. Being ready means different things to different people. Only you know your own emotional timeline. It's not a one-size-fits-all endeavor.

TREAT YOURSELF AND YOUR PARTNERS WITH A LEVEL OF CARE Kindness is key. That means speaking about your body and others' bodies with respect.

NO ONE GETS TO NARRATE THE STORY OF YOUR SEXUALITY BUT YOU Likewise, give others the space to figure out their own trajectory.

That also means you don't get to out folks. Disrupt the notion of the closet. Everyone gets to own their particular experiences on their own schedule.

SEXUALITY IS FLUID You can identify as straight and then identify as pansexual. You can identify as a bisexual and then identify as lesbian. The choices are endless because our experiences and understandings of ourselves evolve over time. Choose, use, and discard labels as they work or don't work. Do you, boo. You make your choices in your own time.

YOU CAN MIX IT UP GENDER-WISE Gender does not mean sexuality. We change and evolve in our gender presentation just as we do in our sexuality.

LIKE WHOMEVER YOU LIKE Just don't let them be raggedy.

MOVIES AND TV

BIG MOUTH

NEVER HAVE I EVER

SEX EDUCATION

TO ALL THE BOYS I'VE LOVED BEFORE

BOOKS

THE ABC'S OF LGBT+ **by Ashley Mardell**

ARE YOU THERE, GOD? IT'S ME, MARGARET **by Judy Blume**

RUBYFRUIT JUNGLE **by Rita Mae Brown**

WE HAVE ALWAYS BEEN HERE: A QUEER MUSLIM MEMOIR **by Samra Habib**

LOVE, INSHALLAH: THE SECRET LOVE LIVES OF AMERICAN MUSLIM WOMEN **by Ayesha Mattu and Nura Maznavi**

REDEFINING REALNESS **by Janet Mock**

ZAMI: A NEW SPELLING OF MY NAME **by Audre Lorde**

UNPROTECTED TEXTS: THE BIBLE'S SURPRISING CONTRADICTIONS ABOUT SEX AND DESIRE **by Jennifer Wright Knust**

SEXUALITY AND THE BLACK CHURCH: A WOMANIST PERSPECTIVE **by Kelly Brown Douglas**

WOMANIST MIDRASH: A REINTRODUCTION TO THE WOMEN OF THE TORAH AND THE THRONE **by Wilda C. Gafney**

FALL TO GRACE: A REVOLUTION OF GOD, SELF & SOCIETY **by Jay Bakker**

IT'S A WRAP

So now you're feminist AF—although from what we know about you, you been on. But now you have some extra tools to make sense of your identity, your home life, your politics, and much more. If you've found something useful in this book and you want your girls to be feminist AF as well, pass along the jewels you've learned.

We know you have a lot going on, not only at home and at school but just in general. It's a lot to take in and to make sense of.

And it's even more important right now that you have tools to understand and navigate the world around you because basically, shit is real.

As we finish this book, COVID-19 has turned the world upside down. Hundreds of thousands of people have died globally. Across the world folks are staying indoors, school has been moved online, and millions are out of work and struggling. The 'Rona has folks running scared, and rightly so. We have had to recalibrate our understanding of society. Even though we aren't sure how things will look on the other side, we do know that our world is forever changed by this experience.

While human beings have retreated inside, the flora and fauna have spread out. Birds seem to be chirping louder than ever now that their melodious tunes aren't drowned out by the sounds of city traffic. Bears, coyotes, mountain lions, and other big animals now emerge during the daytime searching for food without fear of human interference. Cities known for smog, like Los Angeles and Delhi, have reported decreased air pollution, and the Venice canals, long known for their cloudy waters, now run clear. All of this is to say that much of the natural world is taking a breather while humanity waits out this virus.

Some have called these environmental changes a wake-up call, proclaiming that we are the "real virus." But who exactly is this "we"? When there are crowded cities across Asia and Africa, Westerners talk ish about overpopulation without keeping the same energy about the packed streets of London, New York, or San Francisco. There's definitely a double standard when it comes to how Black and Brown "developing" nations are talked about versus the West, despite the fact that countries like the United States are major culprits in pollution, waste, and other environmental calamities.

Hypocrisy aside, the fact of the matter is that things can't really go back to how they were before—not exactly, anyway. This moment of introspection is sort of a test run for some of the extreme measures humanity will have to take to make the planet habitable for the future. The repercussions of COVID-19 will last for years to come, and the fight to combat climate change is humanity's charge for the next several decades.

You were born into a world that—if we're keeping it all the way real—didn't do a good job of preparing a way for you. You have every right to be angry about this, but we hope you will also channel that rage into a vision of a new world, one that is better and more just for the generations to come. As you come of age, you'll be on the vanguard of coming up with solutions of how to live virus-free, develop renewable energy, and create more just societies. Lowkey, it's both daunting and exciting. There are already a slew of young people driving this movement. Young women like Xiye Bastida, Mari Copeny, Isra Hirsi, Jamie Margolin, Elsa Mengistu, Nadia Nazar, and Greta Thunberg are leading the charge on climate change with intersectional activist agendas.

Being feminist AF invites you to cultivate a relationship to the environment and the Earth that rejects the super-masculinist perspective that pervades our current society. Ecofeminism is a branch of feminism that focuses on feminist principles in human beings' relationships to the land, water, air, and overall environment. It sees the Earth is not just a place where we mine and pillage resources, a place to grab and steal from. A feminist relationship to the planet is justice-oriented, reciprocal, and takes into account systems of power like racism, sexism, classism, and imperialism in how we think about land, water, and air. As a feminist, you have the power to help recalibrate our understanding of our relationships to one another and to the Earth.

Still, while there's a lot of work to be done out there, we encourage you to know that some of the most important work happens "in here," at home, in our own communities, and within ourselves. As writer and activist Toni Cade

Bambara once said, "If your house ain't in order, you ain't in order." It's hard to change the world if we don't have our proverbial house in order. That doesn't mean we have to be perfect, it just means we have to strive to be just in all we do with ourselves, our families, and our crews. The personal is always political.

In this moment, your crew is more important than ever. The homies who are your sounding boards and accountability partners, the ones who roast one another in the group chat, the friends whose shoulders you can lean on are what get you through everything from a global pandemic to a breakup to sophomore year. You are never alone. You have a feminist crew of girls and women who care about you and have your back.

ACKNOWLEDGMENTS

BRITTNEY _____

Thanks to my crunk sistren Susana and Chanel. The journey has been a pleasure. Thank you to the Crunk Feminist Collective, where this all began. Thank you to Tanya McKinnon and Carol Taylor at McKinnon Literary for your expansive vision of how Black girls can write the world. Thank you to my play niece Camryn Tims for reading and giving us great feedback on this book. And thank you to Simon Boughton, the Norton Young Readers team, and Amy Medeiros for believing in us and this book.

CHANEL _____

Since this is my first book, I'm about to thank everybody. To my co-writers, Brittney and Susana. Thank you for making this such an incredible and enjoyable journey. Thank you to our agent, Tanya McKinnon, Carol Taylor, and the McKinnon Literary team, and to our editor, Simon Boughton, and everyone at Norton Young Readers, for supporting our vision and making sure this book looked, sounded, and felt like us. This book is for my sweet, fierce, dope little girl, Cori Rain. When you told me you were a feminist, I vowed to do everything in my power to raise you with feminist principles. I wrote this book for a future you and for a past me. Thank you for being my muse. To Cherise and Destiny, because y'all filled my girlhood with so much joy and adventure. I love you dearly. To my little "sisters" Zoe, Alex, Jalena, and Kiyanna. This book is full of all of our car rides, convos, text messages, and late-night couch sessions. It was fun helping you navigate your girlhoods. Thank you for trusting me with your secrets. I am so proud of the women you have become. To all the little girls in my life, especially Rylei Jai, Eila, Brooke-Lynn, Asali, London, and the Junior Feminists Book Club. You remind me every day that girls can do anything if the rest of us would get out of your way. I believe in the power of collectivity, so I have to thank my crews. Thank you to my Center for Women at Emory crew. We've carved out a space of love and possibility while still being "lowkey that bitch." To my Belonging and Community Justice crew for making me believe that another university is possible. To Nuevo, the Cool Kids, and the Ratchet Feminist Trio for showing me the power of friendships and chosen family. And to all my boys especially Mekhi, Jesiah, CJ, Chance, Ayden, Blair, and of course my energetic, brilliant, loving mama's boy Cairo Justice—may you all find the freedom in feminism. To my Brooklyn and VA family, especially my pops, Auntie Pat, Desmond, Carol, Dexter, and my brother Rashan for always being so proud of me. A special thank-you to my ride-or-die husband, Cordero, for constantly reminding me of who I've always been. Finally, to my mother. I only had you for a breath of time, but the lessons you gave me in girlhood still live with me today.

SUSANA

Thanks to my co-writers, Brittney and Chanel. We put our heads and hearts together and created something wonderful. Special thanks to our agent, Tanya McKinnon, and everyone at McKinnon Literary for always having our backs, and to our editor, Simon Boughton, and everyone at Norton Young Readers for encouraging our vision. And very special thanks to all of our readers. We love you!

GLOSSARY

Ableism A system of social norms, beliefs, and institutional power structures that discriminates against people with physical, mental, cognitive, developmental, or learning disabilities.

Agency The capacity for people to act independently and make their own free choices.

American dream The belief that prosperity is tied to hard work, and that having a good job, a big house, 2.5 children, and a dog is what all Americans should aspire to.

Anti-Blackness A specific set of beliefs and ideas rooted in bias against Black people and Black culture. This can show up as stereotypes or outright hatred. It is more specific than white supremacy because anti-Black ideas can show up among people of color groups too.

Asexuality Having little or no sexual feelings, attractions, or desires. Asexual people are sometimes called Ace or Aces. Aces often desire emotionally intimate or romantic relationships.

Binary Pairs of opposing things, such as light/dark, Black/white, rich/poor, etc. Here we are speaking of gender binaries, which presume that there are only two genders: feminine/masculine (see also **Nonbinary**).

Bodily autonomy The right for you to determine what happens to your own body without coercion or force. It is the belief that you get to do what you want with your own body.

Body positivity Having a positive or good body image regardless of what's considered the ideal representation of beauty. It is about accepting your own body and being happy and proud of your body regardless of its size, shape, and appearance.

Cisgender or Cis When someone's gender identity matches the sex they were assigned at birth. For example, if someone was assigned female at birth and identifies as a woman, they may identify as cis.

Capitalism An economic system where the citizens and not the government own and run businesses and companies. In a capitalist system, property is owned and operated by owners, not the workers, with the main motive being to make profit.

Class A social and structural hierarchy based on wealth or lack of wealth.

Classism A social system that confers power, status, and value on the wealthy while devaluing and discriminating against the poor. It is prejudice against or in favor of people belonging to a particular class.

Code-switching Adjusting your speech, appearance, mannerisms, and the like to better fit them into a social scenario. Code-switching is a performative survival technique people of color sometimes use to navigate hostile spaces.

Colorism A belief system that values lighter-skinned people and devalues dark-skinned people.

Consent The permission for something to happen, or a voluntary agreement to do something. When it comes to intimacy and sex, consent should be clear and enthusiastic.

Ecofeminism A way of understanding and moving through the world that combines ecological and feminist concerns. It is a political and philosophical movement that looks at the damage that the patriarchy has done to both people and the ecosystem.

Feminism A social movement and set of beliefs that aims to tear down the system of male domination known as the patriarchy. Ideally, this movement is also antiracist and anti-elitist.

Gaslighting Communication practices designed to both provoke your discomfort and then make you doubt your right to feel uncomfortable or offended (a partner or friend insults you and you know they did it, and then they say, "Stop being so hypersensitive. It's wasn't a big deal!" This is gaslighting).

Gender vs. Sex Gender is the socially constructed characteristics of women and men, while sex is biologically determined and includes reproductive organs, hormones, and chromosomes. One way to think about it is people are born female, male, or intersex, but learn to be boys or girls.

Gender presentation Also known as gender expression. A person's behavior, interests, and appearance that are often correlated with gender, usually but not always binary notions of femininity or masculinity.

Heterosexism The assumption that heterosexuality is the "normal" sexual orientation. Heterosexism often leads to discrimination and prejudice against LGBTQIA+ folk.

Homophobia Hatred of and discrimination toward gay people.

Internalized oppression (racism, classism, homophobia, sexism, white supremacy) Holding negative beliefs about one's own race, class, or sexuality.

Intersectionality A way of understanding how systems of power, such as white supremacy, capitalism, and patriarchy, interact with one another to make life harder for people who are not white, or rich, or cisgender males. In particular, intersectionality helps us to see how oppressions can be compounded if you occupy multiple nonprivileged spaces based on race, gender, sexuality, ability, etc.

Marginalized The process of being disempowered, left out, and having one's concerns and needs overlooked by those with power.

Misogyny The hatred of women. Misogyny is a cornerstone of sexism.

Misogynoir A term coined by scholar Moya Bailey, this refers specifically to the hatred of

Black women. Misogynoir takes into account the racism, sexism, and other institutional oppressions Black women face.

Nonbinary A spectrum of gender identities that are neither exclusively masculine nor feminine. (See also **Binary**.)

Objectification Reducing or degrading someone to the status of an object. Sexual objectification is treating a person specifically as an object of sexual desire.

Oppression When a single group in society unjustly takes advantage of and exercises power over another group using dominance and subordination.

Patriarchy A society in which men hold the power and women are largely excluded from most of the power and authority.

Polyamory A type of relationship where one can have multiple partners with the consent of all the people involved. Polyamory literally means "many love."

Power The capacity to exert control over others and the ability to decide what is best for others and who will get access to resources.

Privilege Unearned advantages and immunities granted and available to a particular group of people.

Race A social and political construct that divides people into categories based on shared physical characteristics, social qualities, or behavioral differences.

Racism Any prejudice against someone because of their race when those views are enforced by systems of power. Institutional racism is the policies and practices deep-rooted in established institutions that result in exclusion or promotion of designated groups. Antiracism is work that actively opposes racism by advocating for changes that reduce racial inequality.

Reproductive justice According to SisterSong Women of Color Reproductive Justice Collective, reproductive justice is "the human right to maintain personal bodily autonomy, have children, not have children, and parent the children we have in safe and sustainable communities."

Restorative justice A system of justice that focuses on mediation and agreement rather than punishment. It centers individuals and communities who were harmed by a crime and considers what it is they need in order to be OK. It believes that a just response to crime helps the offender own what they did and make it right for those who were harmed. It also involves the community in helping both victim and offender.

Sex positive Having a positive attitude about sex that does not believe consensual sex is shameful and instead believes that sex is healthy and pleasurable. It is about feeling comfortable with one's own sexuality and sexual identity as well as accepting of the sexual behaviors and curiosity of others.

Sexism Prejudice, stereotyping, and/or discrimination on the basis of sex or gender, especially against women and girls.

Social capital Social or cultural capital describes the accumulation of knowledge, behaviors, and skills that a person can tap into to demonstrate their social status or move up in society. Think about social capital like the connections that matter. Someone with a lot of social or cultural capital has connections and knowledge that can lead to employment opportunities, entrepreneurial success, educational attainment, and improved health outcomes. .

Social class A person's overall standing in society based on things like income, occupation, and education level. Some examples of social class include upper-class, upper-middle-class, middle-class, working-class, and poor.

Socialization The process by which we learn the norms, values, habits, and attitudes of a culture or a society. For example, the socialization of a girl may begin when she is born and given a pink blanket and continue throughout childhood with the toys she is given and girl characters she sees on TV.

Trans An umbrella term used to describe people whose gender identity differs from what is usually associated with the sex they were assigned at birth.

White supremacy A racial system that presumes white is the superior race, and by extension, that white people are superior people in terms of intelligence, safety, earning power, and fitness for citizenship assigned at birth.

ABBREVIATIONS

FTP: Fuck the patriarchy

POC: People/person of color

WOC: Women/woman of color

INDEX

ABOUT THE AUTHORS

Brittney Cooper is associate professor of women's, gender, and sexuality studies at Rutgers University. She is an award-winning writer and activist and the author of *Beyond Respectability: The Intellectual Thought of Race Women* and the *New York Times* bestseller *Eloquent Rage: A Black Feminist Discovers Her Superpower*. She is also co-founder with Susana Morris of the Crunk Feminist Collective and co-editor with Susana Morris and Robin Boylorn of *The Crunk Feminist Collection*. Brittney is a frequent commentator for cable news outlets on race, gender, pop culture, and politics, and her writing and commentary has been featured at *Time* magazine, the *New York Times*, the *Washington Post*, *Ebony* magazine, *Essence* magazine, NPR, PBS, and Cosmopolitan.com. She has also been named as one of the nation's most influential African Americans multiple times by TheRoot.com. Louisiana born and raised, Brittney likes her tea sweet, her cake by the pound, and her hip-hop with lots of bass.

Chanel Craft Tanner serves as the director of the Center for Women at Emory, where she also earned her PhD in women's, gender, and sexuality studies. As director, her work focuses on creating programs, events, and learning opportunities that recognize and redress historic and persistent gender inequity at Emory and beyond. She is a member of the Crunk Feminist Collective and her writings are featured in *The Crunk Feminist Collection*. She is also a diversity consultant who helps organizations build inclusive and equitable teams. She is passionate about class oppression, prison abolition, hip-hop culture, and Black feminism. A city girl with a country flair, she calls both Brooklyn, New York, and Danville, Virginia, home. When Chanel is not creating programs and developing future leaders, she's probably at a baseball game with her kids or shopping for new earrings. associate professor of literature, media, and communication at the Georgia Institute of Technology.

Susana M. Morris is a queer Jamaican American writer and associate professor of literature, media, and communication at the Georgia Institute of Technology. She is the author of *Close Kin and Distant Relatives: The Paradox of Respectability in Black Women's Literature*. She is the co-editor, with Brittney C. Cooper and Robin M. Boylorn, of *The Crunk Feminist Collection*, and co-editor, with Kinitra D. Brooks and Linda D. Addison, of *Sycorax's Daughters*, a short story collection of horror written by Black women. She is passionate about Afrofuturism, Black feminism, and climate change. She has written for Gawker, Cosmopolitan.com and Ebony.com, and has also been featured on NPR, HuffPost Live, and in *Colorlines* and *Essence* magazine. When Susana's not reading, writing, or teaching, she's probably baking somebody a cake.